THE MORTGAGE PLAYBOOK

An Insider's Guide to Smarter Home Financing Decisions

RL HESSON

RL Hesson - NMLS# 2192188
Hesson Loans - NMLS# 2696086

Published by Hesson Loans
Franklin, Tennessee
www.HessonLoans.com

ISBN: 979-8-9959036-0-4 (paperback)
ISBN: 979-8-9959036-1-1 (hardcover)
ISBN: 979-8-9959036-2-8 (ebook)

CONTENTS

PART III—From Application to Closing Day

INTRODUCTION

What Most Homebuyers Get Wrong About Mortgages

A buyer once came to me after spending nearly a year trying to improve their credit score before purchasing a home.

They had been told repeatedly that they needed a "perfect" 760 credit score in order to qualify for a good mortgage. So they delayed their home search and focused on paying down small credit cards, adjusting balances, and trying to optimize every detail of their credit profile.

By the time they reached out to me, their score was around 720. They were worried it still wasn't good enough.

When we ran the numbers together, something surprising appeared. The difference between a 720 credit score and a 760 credit score on their loan translated to less than $40 per month.

Meanwhile, during the year they spent waiting for the perfect credit score, home prices in their area had increased by nearly 8 percent.

In other words, the delay had cost them far more than the slightly better interest rate would ever have saved.

We moved forward with the purchase. During the process, I was even able to help increase their score slightly through a rapid rescore, but the real lesson had nothing to do with credit scores.

It had everything to do with how people think about mortgages.

Most buyers believe the mortgage process is about finding perfect conditions. The perfect credit score. The perfect interest rate. The perfect time to buy.

But mortgages are rarely about perfection.

They are about strategy.

And when buyers focus on the wrong variables, they make decisions that quietly cost them far more over time.

Why This Book Exists

For most people, buying a home is the largest financial decision they will ever make. Yet the mortgage process is often surprisingly opaque. Borrowers are expected to evaluate loan programs, interest rates, closing costs, underwriting requirements, and long-term financial implications—all within a system they may only encounter a few times in their lives.

Because of this complexity, many buyers focus on the simplest metric available: the interest rate. But focusing only on rate causes buyers to overlook the bigger financial picture.

Questions like:

- *How much liquidity should you keep after closing?*
- *What loan structure matches how long you expect to own the home?*
- *When does paying points actually make sense?*
- *How should a mortgage fit into your broader financial strategy?*

These questions rarely appear in online mortgage calculators. But they matter.

After structuring thousands of mortgages for buyers across Tennessee and the Southeast, I've seen the same misunderstandings appear again and again. This book was written to close that gap.

Who This Book Is For

This book was written for anyone who wants to understand how mortgages really work.

It's a process most of us only go through a few times in our lives. No wonder it feels confusing, rushed, and full of unfamiliar terminology.

Some readers will be purchasing their first home. Others may already own a home and are preparing to move, refinance, or invest in additional properties. You may be relocating to a new city, upgrading to a larger home as your family grows, or simply wanting to understand how financing decisions affect your long-term financial picture.

Wherever you are in the process, the core ideas are the same.

A mortgage is not just a loan. It affects your savings, your flexibility, and your long-term financial options.

This book probably isn't the right fit if you just want the lowest advertised rate, a quick approval, and no discussion about the bigger picture. That approach is perfectly fine.

But this book was written for buyers who want to think about their mortgage a little differently.

How to Use This Book

You do not need to read this book cover to cover in one sitting. Think of it as a playbook you can return to whenever you have a question about how mortgages work or how to structure your financing.

Each chapter focuses on a specific part of the mortgage decision. Some readers will start at the beginning and read straight through. Others may jump to chapters that address their current situation. Both approaches work.

PART I
Thinking About Mortgages the Right Way

1
WHY I SEE MORTGAGES DIFFERENTLY

I DIDN'T START MY CAREER IN THE MORTGAGE BUSINESS.

The way I think about mortgages today was shaped long before I ever worked in lending—by years spent in data analytics, corporate leadership, entrepreneurship, and real estate investing.

My first real education in how systems work came at Caesars Entertainment, where I started as an intern and eventually led the company's e-Business and Analytics team. Caesars was one of the most sophisticated users of customer analytics in the country. Every part of that business was measured—customer behavior, marketing effectiveness, retention patterns, revenue performance. Decisions weren't based on intuition alone. They were supported by data and constantly refined through analysis.

That environment taught me three lessons that still shape how I approach every mortgage conversation today.

First, systems matter. Businesses that scale successfully have repeatable processes behind them. Second, data tells a story. When you understand the numbers, you can see opportunities and risks that aren't obvious at first glance. Third, incentives drive behavior. When you understand how a system is structured, you understand why the people inside it behave the way they do.

That last one is especially important in the mortgage industry—and we'll come back to it throughout this book.

After Caesars, I went on to serve as Chief Information Officer for a rapidly growing behavioral healthcare company, where I oversaw technology systems and infrastructure during a period of significant expansion. Working inside large organizations taught me how to think about capital allocation, growth strategy, and operational decision-making at scale.

But the education that changed how I think about mortgages most directly didn't happen in a corporate office.

It happened when my wife and I started investing in real estate.

Over the years, we gradually built a portfolio of rental properties—eventually growing it to nearly forty units by 2020. We weren't just helping borrowers secure loans. We were borrowers ourselves, sitting across the table from lenders, making the same decisions about leverage, cash flow, and long-term strategy that every homeowner and investor faces.

That experience changed everything. We learned firsthand how financing structures affect cash flow and risk. We saw how one loan structure could create flexibility while another quietly limited it. And we started to realize that most people—including many mortgage professionals—were thinking about these decisions far too narrowly.

As our real estate investing grew, so did our entrepreneurial interests. Over time, we launched several businesses connected to the real estate ecosystem, including a title company, an insurance company, and a mortgage venture that was later acquired. We also co-founded a real estate brokerage that eventually grew to hundreds of agents across multiple states before being purchased by RE/MAX in 2025.

Eventually, I stepped away from the corporate world entirely. After the acquisition of our initial mortgage venture, I founded Hesson Loans, an independent mortgage brokerage based in Franklin, Tennessee. Today my wife and I both hold our real estate licenses with Compass, while I run Hesson Loans full time as the broker-owner.

People sometimes ask why someone with my background would choose to focus on mortgages. The answer is simple.

Mortgages sit at the intersection of real estate, finance, and strategy. And they're widely misunderstood.

The typical approach is to treat a mortgage as a simple transaction—something you get when you buy a house and forget about after closing. But a mortgage is one of the most powerful financial tools you'll ever use. It affects your liquidity, your investment opportunities, your long-term wealth, and your overall financial flexibility.

My background in analytics and systems thinking means I naturally approach mortgage decisions differently. Instead of focusing only on the payment or the rate, I look at the broader financial picture. *How does this loan fit into your overall balance sheet? What does your income trajectory look like? How long do you realistically expect to own the property? How does the mortgage interact with your other debts, investments, and long-term plans?*

When you start asking those questions, the conversation changes completely. It stops being about chasing the lowest rate and becomes about building a financial structure that actually supports your goals.

Most buyers never get to see the mortgage process from this angle. That's what this book is meant to change.

2

THE MORTGAGE INDUSTRY MOST BUYERS NEVER SEE

MOST HOMEBUYERS ONLY INTERACT WITH THE MORTGAGE INDUSTRY for a few weeks during the home-buying process. They apply for a loan, submit documents, review disclosures, sign closing paperwork, and move into their new home. Once the transaction is finished, they rarely think about the lending system again until the next time they buy or refinance.

Because of that, many borrowers assume the mortgage process is fairly simple. You go to a lender. The lender offers a rate. You compare it to another lender's rate. Then you choose the lowest one.

If the mortgage industry actually worked that way, things would be much easier. But behind the scenes, the lending system is more complex than most buyers realize. Multiple institutions are involved, loans are often sold after closing, and pricing can vary based on factors that borrowers rarely see.

You don't need a finance degree to understand this. But knowing the basics will change how confidently you navigate the process.

The Secondary Mortgage Market

When a lender funds a mortgage at closing, that loan is typically sold into what is known as the secondary mortgage market shortly afterward.

Large investors purchase pools of mortgages and package them into mortgage-backed securities, which are then sold to institutional investors around the world. Think of it as bundling thousands of mortgages together and selling shares of that bundle to large investors—much like a mutual fund, but backed by home loans instead of stocks. Those investors might include pension funds, insurance companies, banks, and other large financial institutions that are looking for relatively stable, long-term investment returns.

While this process happens far behind the scenes, it plays a major role in how mortgage rates are determined. Mortgage pricing ultimately flows from the bond market.

When investors are willing to buy mortgage-backed securities at higher prices, mortgage rates tend to fall. When investors demand higher yields in order to purchase those securities, mortgage rates tend to rise.

This is why mortgage rates can change daily—and sometimes even multiple times in a single day.

Most borrowers assume mortgage rates are set by individual lenders. In reality, lenders are largely responding to broader movements in the financial markets.

Why Different Lenders Quote Different Rates

Even though mortgage pricing is influenced by the broader bond market, borrowers often receive slightly different quotes from different lenders.

That can feel confusing. *After all, if two lenders are offering the same type of loan to the same borrower, shouldn't the rate be identical?*

Not necessarily.

Each lender has its own operational costs, pricing models, and risk tolerances. Some lenders operate with larger overhead structures. Others run leaner operations. In addition, lenders often specialize in different areas of the mortgage market. Some focus heavily on jumbo loans. Others specialize in government-backed loans such as FHA or VA. Some lenders are particularly strong with self-employed borrowers or unique income structures.

Because of these differences, one lender may view a borrower's situation as very straightforward while another sees it as more complicated. Once you understand that lenders operate within different business models, the variation starts to make more sense.

Retail Lenders versus Mortgage Brokers

Most borrowers encounter one of two types of lenders during the home-buying process: retail lenders or mortgage brokers.

Retail lenders include large banks, credit unions, and mortgage companies that originate loans using their own lending platforms. When you work with a retail lender, you are typically working within that lender's specific set of products, guidelines, and pricing.

Mortgage brokers operate differently. Instead of lending their own money, brokers work with a network of wholesale lenders that actually fund the loans. The broker's role is to evaluate the borrower's financial situation and match them with the lender and loan structure that best fits their needs.

One way to think about this difference is to compare it to shopping. Working with a retail lender is similar to walking into a single store. Working with a broker is more like working with an advisor who can access multiple stores and help you compare different options.

There's no single correct choice between the two. But they operate differently, and that difference can influence both the loan options available and the advice borrowers receive.

The Gatekeeper Most Buyers Misunderstand

Underwriting is the stage where the lender evaluates the borrower's financial profile to determine whether the loan meets the required guidelines.

This evaluation typically includes reviewing credit history, income documentation, assets and reserves, employment history, and existing debt obligations.

Many buyers imagine underwriting as a mysterious process happening somewhere behind the curtain. In reality, underwriters are simply applying a set of guidelines designed to assess risk. Those guidelines come from a combination of sources, including investor requirements, regulatory standards, and the lender's own internal policies.

But underwriting isn't just about whether you qualify. It's about how clearly your financial story is documented.

Two people with very similar financial profiles can have completely different underwriting experiences depending on how their income, assets, or employment history are structured. This is exactly why preparation matters so much.

What Changes When You See How It All Connects

The biggest takeaway here is that the mortgage industry is not as simple as comparing two interest rates.

Behind every loan quote is a system of lenders, investors, guidelines, and pricing structures. Most buyers never see that system. They just see the final number.

But when you understand how the system works, you ask better questions, evaluate your options more clearly, and make decisions that actually serve your financial goals.

3
THE BIGGEST MISTAKES HOMEBUYERS MAKE

IF YOU ASK MOST BORROWERS WHAT MATTERS MOST WHEN CHOOSING a mortgage, the answer is usually the same: the interest rate.

It's understandable why people focus on that number. Mortgage rates are easy to compare, easy to quote, and easy to understand on the surface. When buyers speak with multiple lenders, the first question is almost always: *"What's your rate?"*

But I've seen buyers choose a lender quoting a slightly lower rate only to discover that the upfront costs required to get that rate made it the most expensive option on the table—especially when they moved within a few years and never recovered those costs.

Situations like this happen more often than people realize.

After working with thousands of borrowers over the years, I've learned something surprising. The biggest mistake most homebuyers make is evaluating the mortgage in isolation—focusing on the rate and the payment without considering how the loan interacts with everything else in their financial life.

Those numbers matter. But they don't tell the whole story—which is why stepping back and looking at how the loan fits into your overall finances changes the conversation. Your mortgage interacts with every other part of your financial life—your liquidity, your debt structure, your investments, and your long-term plans.

We'll explore why chasing the lowest rate can backfire in detail later in the book. But the deeper issue is about perspective.

When the Damage Is Already Done

Not every story in this book ends with a better outcome. Some of the most important lessons come from buyers I met after the decisions had already been made.

A few years ago, a homeowner reached out to me about refinancing. He and his wife had purchased a home about eighteen months earlier through a large national lender. At the time, they had done everything they thought they were supposed to do. They put 20 percent down to avoid mortgage insurance. They stretched to the top of their approval range because their lender assured them they qualified. And they paid nearly $14,000 in discount points to lock in what their lender described as an exceptional rate.

On paper, every individual decision looked responsible.

But eighteen months later, the picture was very different. The large down payment had wiped out most of their savings. Within the first year, their HVAC system failed and their roof needed emergency repairs—roughly $22,000 in unexpected costs they had to put on credit cards because they had no cash reserves. The mortgage payment at the top of their approval range left very little room to pay down that new debt. *And the discount points they had paid to secure the lower rate?* Rates had actually dropped since their purchase. They could have refinanced into a better rate without ever having spent that money.

By the time we spoke, they were carrying more debt than when they had started, their monthly cash flow was tighter than it had been as renters, and the financial flexibility they had spent years building was gone.

No single decision had been obviously wrong in isolation. But together, they created a financial structure with no margin for the unexpected. And homeownership always brings the unexpected.

We were able to help with a refinance that improved their situation. But the conversation would have been very different if someone had looked at the complete financial position before the original purchase—not just the rate, not just the payment, but how every piece fit together.

That's the difference between checking a box and building a financial structure that actually holds up.

The Question Nobody Thinks to Ask

To understand why this matters, it helps to step back and think about your mortgage as part of your overall financial balance sheet.

Your balance sheet includes everything you own and everything you owe: your home, your savings, your investments, your debts, and your monthly cash flow. The mortgage decision sits right in the middle of that system.

Yet most people evaluate it in isolation. They try to minimize the mortgage payment without thinking about how that choice affects everything else.

Instead of asking *"How can I get the lowest payment?"* a better question might be *"How should this mortgage fit into my broader financial picture?"* That shift in perspective can lead to dramatically different decisions.

The $500,000 That Almost Went to the Wrong Place

A couple in Franklin had just sold their home and were sitting on roughly $500,000 in cash. Their plan seemed straightforward. They wanted to put the entire $500,000 toward the purchase of their next home, which was priced around $900,000. Their goal was simple: reduce the mortgage balance as much as possible so they could keep their monthly payment around $2,500.

At first glance, that approach sounds very responsible. Lower debt usually feels like the safest choice.

But when we reviewed their full balance sheet, another detail quickly stood out. They were carrying more than $300,000 in high-interest consumer debt. Between credit cards and other obligations, those debts were costing them roughly $5,000 per month in payments.

If they had followed their original plan—putting the entire $500,000 toward the home—their new mortgage payment would have been about $2,500 per month, but they would still be paying $5,000 each month toward high-interest debt. Their total monthly debt payments would have been around $7,500 per month.

Instead, we explored a different strategy.

Rather than putting the entire $500,000 toward the home purchase, they used about $300,000 of the proceeds to eliminate the high-interest debt completely. The remaining $200,000 went toward the down payment on the new home.

This resulted in a higher mortgage payment—about $4,400 per month instead of $2,500. But the $5,000 in high-interest debt payments disappeared entirely. Their total monthly debt payments dropped from roughly $7,500 to about $4,400.

More importantly, they replaced debt that was costing them between 10 and 30 percent interest with a mortgage costing closer to 5 percent.

The result was dramatically better cash flow and a much stronger financial position. Without looking at the entire balance sheet, that opportunity would have been missed.

The Shift That Changes Everything

The biggest shift in thinking happens when borrowers stop asking *"What's the lowest payment?"* and start asking *"How does this loan fit into my financial life?"*

Once you begin looking at the entire system—your assets, debts, liquidity, and long-term plans—you start asking better questions. And better questions lead to better decisions.

In the chapters ahead, we'll explore many of the specific decisions that shape a mortgage strategy—from down payments and loan programs to underwriting, refinancing, and long-term planning.

PART II
Building Your Mortgage Foundation

4

PREPARING FOR A MORTGAGE 6–12 MONTHS BEFORE BUYING

MANY BUYERS BEGIN THINKING ABOUT FINANCING ONLY AFTER they start touring homes. But the most prepared buyers often begin the process months earlier.

Six to twelve months before applying is the ideal time to strengthen your financial profile. Small adjustments during this window can meaningfully improve your loan options when you're ready to buy.

Reviewing Your Credit

Credit scores affect your mortgage pricing. Perfection isn't required, but even small improvements can reduce your borrowing costs.

During this preparation window, buyers should review their credit reports carefully and look for any inaccuracies or outdated information. Reducing high credit card balances can also improve both credit scores and debt-to-income ratios. These adjustments often take time to reflect on credit reports, which is why planning ahead can be valuable.

Why That New Car Can Wait

Large balances or new loans can increase your debt-to-income ratio and reduce the amount you qualify to borrow. If you plan to buy a home in the near future, it may be wise to avoid taking on new debt whenever possible.

Even relatively small purchases—such as financing furniture, opening a new credit card, or buying a car—can influence how a lender views your financial profile. Many buyers are surprised to learn that major purchases made shortly before applying can sometimes affect their approval.

The Myth That Keeps Buyers from Comparing Lenders

Many buyers worry that shopping for a mortgage will hurt their credit score because of multiple credit inquiries. This concern often prevents people from comparing lenders—which can actually cost them money.

Here's what you should know: when you're shopping for a mortgage, the credit bureaus recognize that you're rate shopping, not taking on multiple new debts. Multiple mortgage-related inquiries made within a focused window—typically fourteen to forty-five days depending on the scoring model—are generally treated as a single inquiry for scoring purposes.

In other words, comparing two or three lenders within a short period will not meaningfully affect your credit score. Don't let this myth prevent you from making an informed decision.

The Job Change That Can Derail a Mortgage

Lenders value consistency. Stable employment and predictable income help demonstrate the borrower's ability to repay the loan.

If you are considering a career change, moving to a commission-based role, or transitioning to self-employment, discussing the timing with a lender beforehand can help avoid surprises.

The Paperwork That Saves You Weeks

Mortgage approvals rely heavily on documentation. Typical documents include recent tax returns, pay stubs, bank statements, and investment account statements. Having these organized early allows your lender to evaluate your financial profile more efficiently.

The Cushion That Changes Everything

Reserves provide reassurance that borrowers can continue making payments even if unexpected expenses arise. In addition to saving for the down payment and closing costs, maintaining liquidity after the purchase can make the transition into homeownership much more comfortable.

It's also helpful to keep documentation for any unusually large deposits that appear on your bank statements. Underwriting guidelines often require lenders to verify the source of significant deposits.

The Buyer Who Was Ready When It Mattered

A couple reached out to me about nine months before they planned to buy. They weren't in a rush—they just wanted to make sure they were in the best possible position when they found the right home.

During that window, we reviewed their credit together and identified a few small adjustments. One credit card had a balance sitting at about 70 percent of its limit, which was dragging their score down more than they realized. By paying it down below 30 percent—not even paying it off entirely—their score improved by nearly 25 points within two months.

We also talked through their savings strategy. They had been putting everything into a single savings account earmarked for the down payment. Instead, we mapped out a plan that covered their target down payment, estimated closing costs, and a comfortable reserve for after closing. Having those three numbers separated made it much easier for them to track their progress and avoid the trap of draining everything into the home.

When they found the right home nine months later, the process moved fast. Their documentation was already organized. Their credit was in an excellent tier. Their reserves were exactly where we had planned. From the time they went under contract to the day they closed, there were no surprises and no scrambling.

Most of the work that made their closing smooth didn't happen during the thirty days between contract and closing. It happened during the nine months before they ever made an offer.

Preparation Creates Opportunity

Buyers who prepare months in advance almost always have better options. Better credit, lower debt, and organized documentation make the process smoother and often unlock better pricing.

5

HOW TO CHOOSE THE RIGHT MORTGAGE ADVISOR

WHEN MANY BORROWERS BEGIN THE MORTGAGE PROCESS, THEIR first instinct is to compare interest rates. While rates are important, they are only one part of the equation.

The person helping structure your loan can have just as big an impact on the outcome.

Why All Lenders Don't See the Same Solutions

Mortgage guidelines are complex, and every borrower's financial situation is different. Experienced advisors have typically worked through a wide range of scenarios—self-employed borrowers, relocations, appraisal challenges, investment properties, and unique income structures.

That experience lets them spot solutions that less experienced lenders miss.

The Calls You Should Be Getting Before Problems Appear

The mortgage process involves many participants—buyers, sellers, agents, underwriters, processors, and title companies. Clear communication among these parties helps keep transactions moving smoothly.

A strong advisor keeps you informed about timelines, documentation requests, and potential issues before they become problems.

One Menu versus the Whole Market

Some lenders work within a single set of loan programs, while others have access to a broader network of lending partners.

If your situation is straightforward, you may not notice a big difference. But if your situation is more complex, having someone who can access multiple loan solutions matters.

The Lender Who Missed the Obvious Solution

A buyer came to me after a frustrating experience with a well-known national lender. She was a nurse who had recently transitioned from a staff position to a travel nursing contract. Her income had actually increased significantly, but because the new role was contract-based rather than salaried, the previous lender told her she would need to wait two full years before her income could be used to qualify.

She was understandably discouraged. She had been planning this purchase for months, her credit was strong, and she had substantial savings. The only thing that had changed was the structure of her income—not the amount.

When we reviewed her situation, the answer wasn't complicated. We worked with a lender that offered a loan program designed for borrowers with non-traditional income documentation. By using her contract and a history of deposits that supported her earning level, we were able to qualify her without waiting two years.

She closed on her home within forty-five days. The previous lender wasn't wrong about their own guidelines—they simply didn't have access to the program that fit her situation. The difference wasn't one lender being good and the other being bad. It was that one had a broader set of tools available.

That distinction matters more often than people realize.

The Conversation That Changes the Outcome

Some lenders focus primarily on processing loans as efficiently as possible. Others take a more strategic approach, helping borrowers evaluate how their mortgage fits into their overall financial strategy.

When lenders take the time to understand a borrower's goals, the conversation changes. Instead of focusing only on interest rates, the discussion becomes about how long you expect to own the home, how much liquidity you should maintain, how your income might change, and how the mortgage interacts with your other financial goals.

Questions Worth Asking Before You Commit

Most borrowers evaluate lenders by asking about rates. But the questions that reveal the most about a lender have nothing to do with pricing.

Before you commit to working with someone, consider asking a few of these:

- *How many loan programs do you have access to?* A lender who works with a single bank or lending platform can only offer what's on their shelf. A lender with access to multiple wholesale partners can shop across a broader set of options. This matters most when your situation isn't perfectly straightforward.

- *What happens if my situation changes during the process?* Job changes, large deposits, appraisal issues, and unexpected credit events happen more often than people expect. A lender who has navigated these situations before will have a plan. A lender who hasn't may freeze—or worse, tell you the deal is dead when it isn't.
- *How will you communicate with me during the process?* This sounds simple, but it matters enormously. Some lenders are proactive—reaching out before deadlines, flagging potential issues early, and keeping you informed at every stage. Others go quiet between application and closing and surface only when they need something from you. Ask how often you'll hear from them and what to expect at each step.
- *Can you walk me through how you'd structure my loan and why?* This is the most revealing question on the list. A lender focused only on transactions will quote a rate and move on. A lender thinking strategically will ask about your timeline, your liquidity, your long-term plans, and then explain how those factors shaped their recommendation. If the lender can't explain *why* they're recommending a specific structure, that tells you something.

You don't need to ask all of these in a single conversation. But paying attention to how a lender responds—whether they answer with depth or deflect with generalities—will tell you far more than any rate quote.

The Test That Tells You Everything

After asking questions and having a few conversations, the decision often comes down to something simple. *Do you trust this person to guide you through one of the largest financial decisions of your life?*

The best mortgage advisor is someone who is knowledgeable, transparent, and willing to explain the reasoning behind every recommendation. They should make you feel comfortable asking questions—even ones that feel basic. And they should be as interested in understanding your financial goals as they are in closing the loan.

When that trust is there, the whole process becomes far more productive. When it isn't, no rate quote in the world makes up for it.

6
THE DOWN PAYMENT DECISION

ASK TEN DIFFERENT HOMEBUYERS HOW MUCH MONEY THEY NEED for a down payment, and many of them will give the same answer: 20 percent.

For years, that number has been repeated so often that many buyers assume it's a requirement for purchasing a home. But the reality is much more flexible. Many homebuyers today purchase homes with far less than 20 percent down. The right choice depends on your financial situation, your goals, and your overall strategy.

Where the "20-Percent Rule" Came From

The idea of putting 20 percent down didn't come from nowhere.

Historically, lenders viewed 20 percent equity as an important risk threshold. Borrowers who put that much money down were statistically less likely to default, and lenders had a stronger equity cushion if something went wrong.

That's also why private mortgage insurance exists. PMI protects lenders when borrowers put down less than 20 percent, covering part of the lender's risk if the borrower defaults.

Over time, the 20 percent threshold became less of a guideline and more of a cultural rule. Parents told their children. Financial articles repeated the advice. And many buyers came to believe that anything less than 20 percent meant they were doing something wrong.

But the mortgage market has evolved significantly. Today many well-qualified buyers choose down payments of 3, 5, or 10 percent, depending on their financial situation. The key isn't blindly following a rule. It's understanding what the tradeoffs actually are.

The Real Risk: Becoming House-Rich and Cash-Poor

One of the biggest risks I see is buyers draining nearly all of their savings into the purchase of their home, leaving almost nothing afterward.

Liquidity, simply put, is your access to cash. It's the money available for emergencies, repairs, opportunities, or unexpected changes in life.

When you drain your liquidity to maximize the down payment, you reduce your financial safety net at the exact moment you're taking on the biggest responsibility of homeownership. And homeownership always comes with surprises. Roofs fail. HVAC systems break. Appliances die. Life happens.

Once your cash becomes home equity, getting it back means selling the property or taking out another loan. That takes time and depends on market conditions. Cash, on the other hand, is immediately available.

What $90 a Month Actually Costs

A first-time buyer in Nashville had spent years saving for a 20 percent down payment. By the time we connected, they were ready to hand over nearly every dollar they had in order to avoid PMI.

Like many buyers, they had heard that putting 20 percent down was the "right" thing to do. From their perspective, paying PMI felt like throwing money away.

So we walked through the numbers together.

Instead of putting 20 percent down, we looked at a five percent down payment option. The monthly PMI payment came out to about $90.

At first, that number confirmed their concerns. *Why pay $90 a month for something that could be avoided?*

But then we looked at what keeping that cash actually meant.

By choosing the smaller down payment, the buyer kept more than $60,000 in reserves instead of putting it entirely into the home. That cash became their financial buffer. It covered renovations they wanted to make after moving in. It provided an emergency fund. It gave them flexibility during the first few years of homeownership.

Meanwhile, it would have taken more than fifty-five years of $90 PMI payments to equal the $60,000 they would have tied up in the home by making the larger down payment. And once their home appreciated and their loan balance dropped, the PMI ended up being removed entirely by year five.

Trying to avoid a small monthly expense would have cost them something much more valuable: financial flexibility.

What Your Options Actually Look Like

Most conventional loans today offer several common down payment structures.

- **3 Percent Down.** Some loan programs allow qualified borrowers to purchase homes with as little as 3 percent down. These programs are often designed for first-time buyers with strong credit and stable income. Because the borrower begins with very little equity, mortgage insurance is required.
- **5 Percent Down.** A 5 percent down payment is one of the most common options for many buyers. It balances a relatively modest upfront investment with manageable monthly mortgage insurance costs. Many buyers find that this option allows them to maintain meaningful cash reserves while still achieving a comfortable monthly payment.
- **10 Percent Down.** At 10 percent down, borrowers reduce both the loan balance and the mortgage insurance cost while still maintaining more liquidity than a 20 percent down payment would allow.
- **20 Percent or More.** Borrowers who put 20 percent down avoid PMI entirely and start with significant equity in the home. For buyers with substantial savings or proceeds from a previous home sale, this can be an attractive option. But larger down payments also tie up more capital inside the property.

When the Rule Actually Applies

This doesn't mean large down payments are always a bad idea.

A larger down payment may be beneficial when the borrower wants to significantly reduce monthly payments, has substantial cash reserves beyond the down payment, the loan structure requires it (such as with some jumbo loans), or the borrower prefers a more conservative leverage strategy.

The key difference is that the decision is intentional, not automatic.

Three Questions That Make the Decision Clearer

When evaluating down payment options, three questions often make the right decision much clearer:

1. *What monthly payment feels comfortable?*
2. *How much liquidity do I want to maintain after closing?*
3. *How long do I expect to own this home?*

Some buyers prioritize lower monthly payments. Others prioritize maintaining flexibility and keeping more cash available. Neither approach is inherently right or wrong. The key is that the decision should align with your broader financial strategy—not simply follow a "rule of thumb" that someone heard years ago.

When the Down Payment Comes from Family

For many first-time buyers, part of the down payment comes as a gift from a parent or close family member. This is perfectly acceptable under most loan programs—but there are specific documentation requirements that catch buyers off guard if they aren't prepared.

Lenders need to confirm that gift funds are truly a gift and not a loan that will need to be repaid. Typically, the person giving the gift will need to provide a signed gift letter stating the amount, their relationship to the borrower, and confirming that no repayment is expected. The lender may also ask for documentation showing the funds leaving the donor's account and arriving in the borrower's account.

Different loan programs have different rules about how much of the down payment can come from gift funds. Some conventional loans require the borrower to contribute a portion from their own savings, while FHA and VA loans are generally more flexible about allowing the entire down payment to come from a gift.

If you expect to use gift funds, discuss this with your lender early in the process. Knowing the requirements ahead of time avoids delays during underwriting.

7

JUST BECAUSE YOU'RE APPROVED DOESN'T MEAN YOU SHOULD BORROW IT

ONE OF THE MOST EXCITING MOMENTS IN THE HOME-BUYING process is receiving a mortgage pre-approval.

For many buyers, it's the moment everything starts to feel real. The numbers are on paper; the search for a home becomes more focused, and buyers finally know how much they can spend.

But here's something most people misunderstand about mortgage approvals: the number a lender approves you for is not a recommendation. It's simply the maximum amount you can technically qualify for under current guidelines. It tells you nothing about how that loan fits into the rest of your balance sheet.

That distinction matters more than you'd think.

How Lenders Decide What You Can Borrow

When lenders calculate your approval amount, they rely heavily on something called a debt-to-income ratio, often abbreviated as DTI.

This ratio measures how much of your monthly income goes toward debt obligations, including your potential mortgage payment. For example, if a household earns $10,000 per month and has total monthly debt payments of $4,000, their debt-to-income ratio would be 40 percent.

Most loan programs allow borrowers to qualify with a DTI ratio up to around 50 percent, and sometimes even higher depending on the loan program and credit profile.

In other words, a lender may approve you for a payment that consumes nearly half of your gross monthly income. From a technical underwriting standpoint, that may be acceptable. From a lifestyle standpoint, it may not be ideal.

Approved Doesn't Mean Comfortable

The approval process is designed to answer one specific question: *Can the borrower reasonably repay this loan?*

But that's a very different question from: *Will this loan support the borrower's lifestyle and long-term financial goals?*

I've worked with plenty of buyers who were approved for payments far higher than what they actually felt comfortable with.

For example, imagine a household earning a strong income that qualifies for a mortgage payment of $5,500 per month. On paper, the numbers work. But after talking through their financial priorities, the buyers realized that a payment closer to $4,000 per month would allow them to maintain a lifestyle they enjoy. That extra $1,500 per month could go toward travel, investing, savings, children's activities, or simply financial flexibility.

When you stretch to the maximum, those choices disappear.

The $950,000 Home They Decided Not to Buy

A couple relocating to the Nashville area were surprised by how much they were approved to borrow.

Based on their income, the lender's automated approval system indicated they could comfortably qualify for a home priced around $950,000. At first, they assumed that meant they should be looking at homes in that range.

But when we walked through their finances as a whole, the conversation changed. They enjoyed traveling several times each year. They were contributing aggressively to retirement accounts. They also hoped to begin investing in rental properties within the next few years.

When we calculated the payment on a $950,000 purchase, the mortgage would have required roughly $5,700 per month.

Technically, they qualified. But when we compared that number to their long-term goals, they realized a home priced closer to $725,000 would leave significantly more room in their budget for investing, travel, and future opportunities.

They ultimately purchased the less expensive home.

A few years later, they told me it was one of the best financial decisions they had made. The lower payment gave them the flexibility to invest in two rental properties and maintain the lifestyle they wanted. As a bonus, those rental properties brought in over $70,000 per year in net income.

The Number Your Lender Won't Question

There's another detail worth understanding: lenders evaluate **gross income**, not how you actually spend your money. Gross income is your income before taxes. But you live on **net income**—what's left after taxes, insurance, retirement contributions, and other deductions.

When those factors are considered, the percentage of take-home income going toward housing can be significantly higher than the DTI ratio suggests. That's why two families with identical incomes can experience the same mortgage payment very differently.

Start with Your Life, Then Find the House

Instead of asking how much house you can afford, ask a better question: *How much house do you want to afford?*

That shift lets you build a financial structure that supports your life rather than dominating it.

One helpful exercise is to start with your overall financial priorities and work backward:

- *What does your ideal monthly financial life look like?*
- *How much do you want to allocate toward housing?*
- *How much do you want to invest each month?*
- *How much flexibility do you want to maintain?*

Once those numbers are clear, it becomes much easier to determine the home price that fits comfortably within that structure. Your home should enhance your life—not quietly limit it.

Co-Borrowers and Co-Signers

During the mortgage process, some buyers consider adding another person to the loan—either as a co-borrower or a co-signer. These terms are often used interchangeably, but they mean different things, and the distinction matters.

A co-borrower is a full participant in the loan. They share responsibility for the mortgage, and they typically also go on the title to the property. Both borrowers' income, assets, and credit are used in the qualification process. This is the most common arrangement for married couples or partners purchasing a home together.

A co-signer, on the other hand, takes on responsibility for the debt but does not go on the title. They're essentially guaranteeing the loan. Their income and credit help the primary borrower qualify, but they have no ownership interest in the property.

Co-signers are most common when a parent helps an adult child qualify for a mortgage. The parent's income or credit strengthens the application, but the child is the sole owner of the home.

Both arrangements carry real financial implications. The co-borrower or co-signer is fully liable for the mortgage. If the primary borrower stops making payments, the co-signer or co-borrower is responsible—and the missed payments will affect their credit as well.

For the co-signer and co-borrower, the mortgage also appears as a debt obligation on their credit report, which can affect their own ability to borrow in the future.

These arrangements can be valuable in the right circumstances. But they should be entered into carefully, with a clear understanding of the financial responsibility involved. A conversation with your lender about how adding a co-borrower or co-signer would affect both parties is always a good idea before making that decision.

The $9,500 Payment That Wasn't What It Seemed

On paper, the numbers looked intimidating. A buyer moving from California to Tennessee was staring at a projected payment of roughly $9,500 per month on a $1.5 million home.

She had significant income, a high level of flexibility, and was planning a major life transition. Her daughter was about to get married, she still had financial obligations tied to her home in California, and she wasn't ready to sell that property just yet. She also wanted to keep her down payment relatively low so she could preserve liquidity for other investments.

Then, she started to hesitate.

The payment felt higher than she expected, and she began questioning whether the move made financial sense at all.

At that point, we stepped back and looked at the full picture—not just the mortgage.

She was currently paying California state income tax. Her homeowners insurance was over $18,000 per year. Her property taxes were close to $20,000 annually.

All of those expenses were about to change.

Moving to Tennessee meant no state income tax. Insurance on a similar property would be closer to $2,500 per year. Property taxes in her target area were roughly $3,000 to $5,000 annually.

Those differences reshaped her overall cost structure.

Once we reframed the conversation around total cost of living—not just the mortgage payment—the decision became much clearer.

From there, we adjusted the purchase strategy. Instead of stretching to $1.5 million, we targeted a home closer to $1.2 million and structured the down payment to keep the loan within conventional limits rather than moving into a jumbo loan.

The result was a more comfortable monthly payment, improved loan structure, and a significant reduction in overall annual expenses.

Nothing about her income had changed. But once we looked beyond the mortgage and into her complete financial position, the move made far more sense.

8

WHY THE LOWEST RATE ISN'T ALWAYS THE BEST LOAN

IF YOU ASK MOST BORROWERS WHAT THEY WANT FROM A LENDER, the answer usually comes down to one thing: the lowest possible interest rate.

It makes sense. Mortgages are large loans, and even small rate differences affect the monthly payment. But the assumption that the lowest rate always produces the best outcome is one of the most expensive misunderstandings in the lending process.

A mortgage is not a single number. It's a structure. And that structure includes multiple components that influence how the loan performs over time.

Why "Lowest Rate" Marketing Can Be Misleading

Part of the problem is how mortgages are advertised. Lenders promote the lowest available rate because it's the easiest number to compare and the easiest headline to run.

But those advertised rates frequently assume certain conditions, such as paying discount points, a very specific credit score, a particular loan size, or a certain down payment.

Two loans with the same rate may have very different costs depending on the fees required to obtain that rate. That's why comparing mortgages requires looking at both rate and cost, not just the interest rate alone.

The Role of Discount Points

One of the most common ways lenders create a lower rate is through discount points—upfront fees paid at closing in exchange for a reduced rate. We'll explore how discount points work in detail in Chapter 13, including how to calculate the breakeven period and when paying points actually makes sense.

But the core idea is simple: when a borrower pays money upfront to reduce the rate, those savings only materialize if they keep the loan long enough to recover the cost. When they don't, the "lower rate" turns out to be the more expensive option.

Why the Same Rate Can Cost Two Different Amounts

Even when two lenders quote the same interest rate, the total cost of the loan can be very different.

Every mortgage comes with fees beyond the interest rate—origination fees, underwriting fees, processing fees, and other lender charges. One lender might quote 6.5 percent with $4,000 in total lender fees. Another might quote the same 6.5 percent but charge $9,000. The monthly payment would be identical, but the second loan costs $5,000 more at closing.

This is why borrowers should always compare the full cost of the loan, not just the rate.

One useful tool for this comparison is the APR—the annual percentage rate. The APR takes the interest rate and rolls in most of the lender's fees, expressing the true cost of the loan as a single number. A loan quoted at 6.5 percent with high fees might carry an APR of 6.8 percent, while the same rate with lower fees might show an APR of 6.6 percent.

The APR isn't perfect. It assumes you'll keep the loan for the full term, which most people don't. But it's a quick way to see whether a lower rate is genuinely cheaper or just hiding its cost somewhere else. Your Loan Estimate will include the APR alongside the interest rate—comparing those two numbers across lenders is one of the simplest ways to evaluate competing offers.

The Cost That Doesn't Show Up on the Rate Sheet

There's another factor that rarely gets discussed when borrowers compare rates: the lender's ability to execute.

A slightly lower rate from a lender with slower processing times, rigid underwriting, or poor communication can end up being the most expensive choice a borrower makes—not because of the loan terms, but because of what happens during the transaction.

I've seen buyers choose the lowest-rate lender only to face repeated documentation delays, missed deadlines, and last-minute surprises that nearly derailed their closing. In competitive markets, a delayed closing doesn't just cause stress. It can cost you the home entirely if the seller loses confidence and moves to a backup offer.

Other lenders may not offer rate flexibility that matters during the process—such as the ability to float down to a lower rate if market conditions improve before closing, or the willingness to restructure the loan quickly if something changes in underwriting.

None of these things appear on a rate quote. But they directly affect whether the loan you were promised is the loan you actually receive—and whether you close on time.

The $18,000 They Almost Spent

By the time this buyer came to me, they were about to pay $18,000 in discount points to reduce their rate with a national lender. Their credit profile was strong: excellent credit, stable income, and a substantial down payment.

On the surface, the numbers looked attractive. But when we walked through their long-term plans, they mentioned something important. Their careers made it likely they would relocate again within three to five years.

That detail completely changed the math. The breakeven period on the discount points was more than seven years. If they followed their expected timeline and moved within five years, they would never recover the money they spent to buy down the rate.

Instead, we structured the loan without discount points. The interest rate was slightly higher, but they preserved their liquidity and avoided spending money on something that didn't align with their timeline. That decision will save them roughly $15,000 to $18,000 if they move when they expect to.

The Question That Replaces "What's Your Rate?"

Stop asking *"What's the rate?"* Start asking *"What loan structure fits my situation best?"*

Sometimes the best mortgage structure does involve securing the lowest possible rate. But other times, flexibility matters more. If a borrower expects interest rates to decline in the future, they may intentionally avoid paying points because they anticipate refinancing later. In that situation, preserving cash today may be far more valuable than shaving a small amount off the interest rate.

9

WHAT LENDERS ACTUALLY LOOK FOR

FOR MOST BUYERS, UNDERWRITING FEELS LIKE THE MOST MYSTERIOUS part of the mortgage process. Documents get requested. More information is needed. Conditions appear. It can feel like your entire financial life is suddenly under a microscope.

But it's actually much simpler than it feels.

At its core, underwriting is simply the process lenders use to answer one question: *Can this borrower reasonably repay the loan?*

To answer that question, lenders evaluate four primary areas of a borrower's financial profile. These are often referred to as the **Four C's of Lending**: Credit, Capacity, Capital, and Collateral.

Credit: Your Financial History

Credit is one of the first things lenders evaluate. Your credit report provides a record of how you've handled debt in the past—whether payments have been made on time, how much debt you currently carry, and how long you've been using credit.

Credit scores summarize this information into a number, typically ranging from 300 to 850. Most conventional loan programs require a minimum score in the low-to-mid 600s, while FHA loans may accept scores as low as 580 with a 3.5 percent down payment.

But once your credit score reaches a strong range, small differences matter far less than you'd expect. In many loan programs, borrowers are grouped into pricing tiers. A borrower with a 740 and a borrower with a 758 will often receive the same rate. The meaningful pricing jumps tend to happen at thresholds like 680, 700, 720, 740, and 760—not at every single point along the scale.

You may already be in a stronger position than you think. A quick conversation with a knowledgeable lender early on can clarify where you stand, what tier you fall into, and whether a small adjustment—like paying down a credit card balance—could move you into a better pricing band before you apply.

Capacity: Your Ability to Repay

Capacity measures your ability to make the monthly mortgage payment based on your income and existing debt obligations. This is where your DTI (the debt-to-income ratio we mentioned in Chapter 7) comes into play.

Your DTI compares your total monthly debt payments to your gross monthly income. Lenders look at two versions of this ratio. The front-end ratio considers only your proposed housing costs—mortgage payment, property taxes, insurance, and any HOA fees. The back-end ratio includes your housing costs plus all other recurring debt obligations—car payments, student loans, credit card minimums, and any other monthly debts.

For example, if a household earns $10,000 per month and has $3,500 in total debt payments including the proposed mortgage, their back-end DTI would be 35 percent.

Different loan programs have different thresholds, but many conventional loans allow borrowers to qualify with back-end ratios up to 50 percent. FHA loans can sometimes stretch slightly beyond that with strong compensating factors like significant cash reserves.

As we discussed earlier, qualification doesn't equal comfort. The lender's job is to determine whether you can repay the loan. Your job is to determine whether the payment allows you to live the way you want. Smart buyers pay attention to both.

Capital: Your Financial Resources

Capital refers to the financial resources a borrower brings to the transaction—funds for the down payment, closing costs, and reserves remaining after the purchase.

Lenders want to see that you have enough money to complete the transaction and that you won't be financially depleted the day after closing. The specific reserve requirements depend on the loan program. Some conventional loans require no formal reserves for a primary residence, while others—particularly jumbo loans or investment property loans—may require several months' worth of mortgage payments sitting in verifiable accounts after closing.

Reserves can include checking and savings accounts, retirement accounts, investment portfolios, and in some cases other documented liquid assets. The key is that the funds are verifiable and accessible.

From a lender's perspective, reserves are a safety net. If you hit a rough patch with income, those reserves help you keep making payments. This is why lenders feel more comfortable—and sometimes offer better terms—when you maintain liquidity after closing.

Collateral: The Property Itself

In a mortgage transaction, the home itself serves as the **collateral** for the loan. The lender needs to confirm that the property has sufficient value to support the amount being borrowed.

That's where the appraisal process comes in. An independent appraiser evaluates the property and compares it to similar homes that have recently sold in the area. If the property appraises at or above the purchase price, the transaction can typically move forward without issue.

Why Preparation Matters

Once you understand these four areas—and how they connect to your overall balance sheet—the mortgage process becomes far less intimidating.

Most underwriting delays happen not because you're unqualified, but because documentation needs clarification. With proper preparation, most of these issues are avoidable.

10

PRE-QUALIFICATION VERSUS PRE-APPROVAL

Why the Difference Matters

BEFORE MOST BUYERS START TOURING HOMES, THEY'LL HEAR THE same advice from real estate agents: *"Get pre-approved first."*

It's good advice. A mortgage pre-approval helps buyers understand what they can afford and signals to sellers that the buyer is serious and capable of completing the purchase.

But **not all pre-approvals are created equal.** The terms **pre-qualification** and **pre-approval** are used interchangeably all the time, even though they represent very different levels of review.

The Quick Estimate That Doesn't Carry Much Weight

A **pre-qualification** is typically the most basic form of loan estimate. It's usually based on information provided verbally by the borrower or entered into an online application. Because the information has not yet been fully verified, the pre-qualification is usually considered preliminary.

Think of it as an **early snapshot**. It's useful when you're just starting to explore, but it won't carry much weight with sellers—especially in a competitive market.

The Review That Actually Opens Doors

A **pre-approval** typically involves a much more thorough review of the borrower's financial situation. Instead of relying only on estimates, the lender reviews actual documentation such as pay stubs, tax returns, bank statements, credit reports, and employment verification.

Once that review is complete, the lender can issue a **pre-approval letter** that reflects a much higher level of confidence in the borrower's ability to qualify.

In some cases, the borrower's file may even be reviewed by an **underwriter** before they begin shopping for a home. This is sometimes referred to as a **fully underwritten pre-approval**. When a buyer reaches this level of preparation, it significantly reduces uncertainty later in the process.

Why This Distinction Can Win or Lose You a Home

From a buyer's perspective, both documents may look similar. But from a seller's perspective, the difference can be substantial.

When a seller accepts an offer, they're taking their home off the market and trust that the buyer's financing will ultimately be approved. If that financing falls apart weeks later, the seller may have lost valuable time and other potential buyers.

Two Lost Offers and a Pre-Approval That Wasn't One

A buyer had already lost out on two homes in competitive situations. They had been working with a large online lender and had what they believed was a strong pre-approval letter.

But when we reviewed their file together, we discovered that the previous lender had issued what was essentially a basic pre-qualification. Their financial documents had never actually been reviewed.

When the listing agent called the lender to verify the strength of the financing, the lender couldn't confidently confirm that the buyer's file had been fully evaluated.

After reviewing the situation, we gathered the buyer's documentation and completed a much more thorough pre-approval review. When the buyer submitted their next offer, the listing agent called me directly to ask about the financing.

Because the file had already been reviewed in detail, I was able to confidently confirm that the buyer's income, assets, and documentation had been fully evaluated. That additional confidence helped the buyer secure the home, even though their offer wasn't the highest.

Sometimes certainty matters almost as much as price.

The Advantage of Showing Up Ready

One of the best things you can do is prepare your financial documentation before you start searching seriously.

A fully reviewed pre-approval doesn't happen by accident. It requires a few specific steps on your part.

First: Expect to provide complete documentation upfront—not just the basics. That typically means your two most recent pay stubs, two years of W-2s or tax returns, two months of bank statements, and any documentation related to additional income sources such as bonuses, rental income, or self-employment earnings.

Second: Be prepared for a credit pull. A pre-approval involves a hard credit inquiry, which gives the lender access to your full credit profile. As we discussed earlier, mortgage-related inquiries within a focused shopping window are generally treated as a single inquiry for scoring purposes, so this should not discourage you from getting properly reviewed.

Third: Respond quickly when your lender asks follow-up questions. Underwriters reviewing your file during the pre-approval process may need clarification on specific deposits, employment gaps, or other details. The faster you respond, the sooner your pre-approval is fully confirmed—and the stronger your position when you're ready to make an offer.

The difference between a casual pre-qualification and a thorough pre-approval is not just the lender's effort. It's yours. Buyers who invest the time upfront consistently find that the rest of the process moves faster, with far fewer surprises—and when the right home appears, they're ready to move with confidence.

PART III

From Application to Closing Day

11
CHOOSING THE RIGHT MORTGAGE PROGRAM

THE MORTGAGE PROCESS COMES WITH ITS OWN VOCABULARY. Terms like **conventional**, **FHA**, **VA**, and **jumbo** start showing up in conversations with lenders, agents, and friends who've bought homes before. These describe different categories of mortgage programs. The details can get complex, but the basics are straightforward.

Most homebuyers will choose from one of four primary loan categories.

Conventional Loans

Conventional loans are the most common type of mortgage used by homebuyers. These loans are not insured by a government agency. Instead, they follow guidelines established by government-sponsored enterprises such as Fannie Mae and Freddie Mac.

They are often a strong fit for borrowers with **stable income, solid credit profiles,** and **moderate to substantial down payments**. Down payments can be as low as 3 percent in some situations, although many borrowers choose to put 5 percent, 10 percent, or more down.

When the down payment is less than 20 percent, private mortgage insurance is typically required. As we discussed earlier, PMI on conventional loans can often be removed once the borrower builds sufficient equity in the home.

Because conventional loans are widely available, relatively flexible, and adaptable to many financial situations, they form the backbone of the mortgage market.

FHA Loans

Loans insured by the Federal Housing Administration are commonly known as FHA loans. These programs were originally designed to make homeownership more accessible, particularly for borrowers who may have smaller down payments or credit profiles that do not meet conventional guidelines.

One of the most well-known features of FHA loans is their **low down payment** requirement. Qualified buyers can often purchase a home with as little as 3.5 percent down. FHA loans also tend to be more forgiving when it comes to credit history.

However, FHA financing includes mortgage insurance requirements that can make the loan more expensive over the long term. For FHA loans with a down payment of less than 10 percent, mortgage insurance remains in place for the life of the loan unless the borrower later refinances into a different program. Borrowers who put 10 percent or more down on an FHA loan will see the mortgage insurance removed after eleven years.

Because of that, some borrowers use FHA financing as a temporary starting point, then refinance into a conventional loan once their equity and financial profile improve.

VA Loans

Loans guaranteed by the U.S. Department of Veterans Affairs are available to eligible military service members, veterans, and certain surviving spouses.

VA loans offer several powerful advantages. Qualified borrowers can frequently purchase a home with **no down payment** and **no monthly mortgage insurance**.

Because the VA guarantees a portion of the loan, lenders are often able to offer competitive interest rates and flexible underwriting standards. For those who qualify, VA loans are often considered one of the most attractive mortgage programs available.

Jumbo Loans

While conventional loans cover a wide range of home prices, there is a maximum loan amount established each year by Fannie Mae and Freddie Mac. This is called the conforming loan limit. As of the time of this writing, the baseline limit is $832,750 in most parts of the country, though it is higher in designated high-cost areas. For example, the conforming limit in Williamson County, Tennessee, is $1,029,250. These limits are updated annually—typically announced each November—so it is worth confirming the current figures with your lender when you begin the process.

Loans that exceed the conforming limit are known as jumbo loans.

Because these loans involve larger balances and greater financial exposure for lenders, the qualification requirements are often somewhat stricter. Borrowers may need credit scores of 700 or higher, down payments of at least 10 to 20 percent, and several months of cash reserves after closing. Interest rates on jumbo loans can sometimes be competitive with conventional rates depending on your down payment, but the underwriting process tends to be more detailed.

For buyers purchasing higher-value homes—which is common in many parts of Tennessee and the Southeast—understanding where the conforming limit falls can influence which loan structure makes the most sense.

USDA Loans

One additional government-backed program that many buyers overlook is the USDA Rural Development loan. These loans are guaranteed by the U.S. Department of Agriculture and are designed to promote homeownership in eligible rural and suburban areas.

Like VA loans, USDA loans offer the **possibility of no down payment**. They also tend to feature **competitive interest rates**. However, they come with income limits—borrowers must fall below a certain household income threshold for the area—and the property must be located in a USDA-eligible zone.

You can check whether a specific property is in a USDA-eligible area by using the USDA's online eligibility map, which is publicly available on their website. It's worth checking early—especially if you're shopping in suburban areas outside a major city, where eligibility boundaries can be surprising. Quite a few suburban communities outside major metro areas qualify, including parts of Tennessee and the Southeast.

USDA loans do require a form of mortgage insurance—called a **guarantee fee**—but it is typically lower than PMI on a conventional loan or mortgage insurance on an FHA loan. For buyers who meet the income and location requirements, USDA financing can be one of the most affordable paths to homeownership.

Programs Most Buyers Never Hear About

There are also additional loan structures designed for specific borrower situations. For example, some lenders offer bank statement loans designed for self-employed borrowers whose tax returns may not fully reflect their true income.

Other programs, such as Debt Service Coverage Ratio loans—commonly called DSCR loans—focus on investment properties. Rather than qualifying the borrower based on personal income, these loans evaluate whether the property's rental income is sufficient to cover the mortgage payment. We'll explore how DSCR loans work in more detail in Chapter 20.

An experienced lender can help you figure out when one of these alternatives makes sense.

The Loan Program Nobody Suggested

She walked in certain she needed a conventional loan. That was what her parents had used, what her coworkers recommended, and what felt like the obvious choice. Her credit score of 660 told a different story.

Her financial profile was average, but not perfect. She had a modest amount of savings, and she was purchasing on her own. When we ran the numbers on a conventional loan, the picture was tight. She was being penalized on the rate for her score and the mortgage insurance suffered as a result.

Then we looked at an FHA loan.

With FHA financing, her down payment was a manageable 3.5 percent. The mortgage insurance was comparable to what the conventional loan required at her credit tier. And because FHA guidelines are more flexible with credit history, the approval process was very straightforward.

But here's the part most lenders skip. We didn't just choose the FHA loan and move on. We built a plan around it.

FHA mortgage insurance generally stays on the loan for its entire life. That's a real cost. Yes, you have an upfront mortgage insurance premium, but with the savings on the rate, we would get that back over time. So, we mapped out a timeline. Over the next three years, she would focus on building equity through normal payments and home appreciation while also improving her credit score. Once she crossed into scoring tiers with smaller penalties—typically a 700 or higher, she could refinance into a conventional loan.

She closed on her home within thirty days. A few years later, we touched base. Her credit score had improved to 760 with our score improvement plan, her home had appreciated during the COVID boom, and she had enough equity to refinance into a conventional loan with no mortgage insurance. Her monthly payment dropped significantly.

The FHA loan wasn't a compromise. It was a starting point. And because we planned the next step from the beginning, she never felt stuck in it.

Why Two Identical Buyers Might Choose Different Loans

Many buyers assume choosing the right loan program is just about qualifying.

In reality, it's a broader conversation about your goals, your liquidity, and your long-term plans. Two buyers with identical financial profiles might choose completely different programs.

The best program isn't the one that looks best on paper. It's the one that fits your actual financial picture.

12

FIXED VERSUS ADJUSTABLE

Choosing the Right Mortgage Structure

FOR MANY HOMEBUYERS, THE THIRTY-YEAR FIXED-RATE MORTGAGE feels like the default choice. It's familiar, predictable, and widely discussed. With a fixed-rate loan, the interest rate remains the same for the entire life of the mortgage, meaning the principal and interest portion of the payment never changes.

But it isn't the only option available.

How Adjustable-Rate Mortgages Work

An adjustable-rate mortgage begins with an initial period where the interest rate is fixed. After that period ends, the rate can adjust periodically based on broader market interest rates.

For example, a 7/1 ARM means the interest rate is fixed for the first seven years and can adjust once per year after that. A 5/1 ARM has a fixed rate for five years before adjustments begin.

During the initial fixed period, the interest rate on an ARM is often lower than the rate offered on a comparable thirty-year fixed mortgage. That lower rate can translate into meaningful payment savings during the early years.

Modern adjustable-rate mortgages also include rate caps, which limit how much the interest rate can increase at the first adjustment, during each future adjustment, and over the life of the loan.

Many borrowers remember negative stories about adjustable-rate mortgages during the housing crisis of the late 2000s. At that time, some borrowers were placed into products with short introductory periods and large potential payment increases.

Today's ARM products are structured very differently. Lending standards are far stricter, and you have to qualify based on much more conservative guidelines.

To see how this works in practice, consider a borrower who takes out a 7/1 ARM on a $500,000 loan at an initial rate of 5.75 percent. Their principal and interest payment during the first seven years would be approximately $2,918 per month.

Now suppose the ARM has a common cap structure of 2/2/5—meaning the rate can increase by a maximum of 2 percent at the first adjustment, up to 2 percent at each subsequent annual adjustment, and no more than 5 percent over the life of the loan.

If market rates have risen by the time the fixed period ends, here is what the worst-case scenario looks like. At year eight, the rate could adjust to 7.75 percent, bringing the payment to roughly $3,571. At year nine, it could rise to 9.75 percent and a payment of approximately $4,234. And the lifetime cap would prevent the rate from ever exceeding 10.75 percent, which on this loan would mean a maximum possible payment of around $4,703.

Those are meaningful increases. But they also represent the ceiling, not the expectation. In practice, adjustments are based on a market index plus a margin, and rates can adjust downward as well as upward. The point of understanding the caps is that you know the worst case before you sign.

For the borrower who expects to sell or refinance within seven years, none of those adjustments would ever come into play. They would simply benefit from the lower rate during the fixed period and move on.

The Buyer Who Saved Thousands by Not Playing It Safe

One of the most important questions borrowers can ask when choosing a mortgage is: *How long do I realistically expect to own this home?*

Many homeowners move or refinance long before thirty years pass. Career changes, family growth, relocations, and lifestyle changes often lead people to sell or refinance within five to ten years.

The buyer's timeline was clear: five to seven years in the home, then a relocation. Her instinct was a thirty-year fixed mortgage—the safe choice. But safe and smart aren't always the same thing.

A seven-year adjustable-rate mortgage offered a significantly lower interest rate. Because the buyer expected to move within that window, the adjustable portion would likely never come into play. Over those seven years, the lower rate would save tens of thousands of dollars compared to the fixed-rate option.

The adjustable-rate mortgage wasn't risky. It simply aligned with the borrower's expected timeline.

Your Mortgage Should Match Your Plans, Not Your Fears

I'm not saying adjustable-rate mortgages are always better. For many people, the stability of a fixed rate provides peace of mind that's worth the slightly higher cost. But your mortgage choice should be intentional. The best mortgage is rarely the one everyone else picks. It's the one that matches your timeline and your strategy.

13
MORTGAGE POINTS AND RATE BUYDOWNS

AT SOME POINT DURING THE MORTGAGE PROCESS, BORROWERS ARE often presented with a choice: accept a certain interest rate with standard closing costs, or pay additional money upfront in order to reduce that rate.

Those upfront costs are called discount points. We touched on this concept briefly when discussing loan pricing, but it's worth exploring in more detail—because the decision of whether to pay points is one of the most consequential choices borrowers make.

What Are Mortgage Discount Points?

A mortgage point is essentially prepaid interest. Borrowers pay money at closing in exchange for a lower interest rate on the loan. In most cases, one point equals 1 percent of the loan amount.

For example, if a borrower takes out a $500,000 mortgage, one point would cost $5,000. In return, the lender reduces the interest rate. Exactly how much the rate decreases depends on market conditions, but the idea is consistent: you pay more today in order to pay less interest over time.

The Math That Decides Whether Points Pay Off

Earlier in the book, we introduced the concept of the breakeven period. Let's look at how that math actually works.

When borrowers pay points, they must remain in the loan long enough for the monthly payment savings to recover the upfront cost.

For example, imagine a borrower pays $6,000 in discount points to reduce their monthly payment by $120.

$6,000 ÷ $120 = 50 months

The borrower would need to keep the loan for a little more than four years before the lower payment actually begins producing net savings. If they sell or refinance before that point, the upfront money is never fully recovered.

This is why your time horizon matters so much. Mortgage decisions should reflect how long you realistically expect to keep the property and the loan.

When Paying Points Can Make Sense

For borrowers who expect to remain in the home for many years, a slightly lower interest rate can produce meaningful long-term savings. Others prefer the certainty of locking in the lowest possible payment. And in some market environments, borrowers may believe interest rates are unlikely to fall significantly in the future.

But more often than not, borrowers benefit more from maintaining flexibility.

When the Pricing Works in Reverse

Borrowers are sometimes surprised to learn that mortgage pricing works in both directions. Just as borrowers can pay points to lower their rate, they can sometimes choose a slightly higher rate in exchange for lender credits.

Lender credits reduce the borrower's upfront closing costs. For buyers who prefer to conserve cash at closing, this structure can sometimes make more sense than paying points.

How We Turned a Slow Market into $500 a Month

In addition to discount points, borrowers may also encounter temporary rate buydowns. Unlike discount points, which permanently reduce the interest rate, temporary buydowns lower the payment for a limited period—typically the first one or two years of the loan.

One of the most common structures is known as a 2-1 buydown. Here's how it works.

Imagine a borrower takes out a $400,000 mortgage with a note rate of 7 percent. The full principal and interest payment at that rate would be roughly $2,661 per month.

With a 2-1 buydown:

- **Year one:** the rate drops to 5 percent, and the payment falls to approximately $2,147—saving about $514 per month.
- **Year two:** the rate adjusts to 6 percent, and the payment becomes roughly $2,398—saving about $263 per month.
- **Year three and beyond:** the rate returns to the original 7 percent, and the payment settles at the full $2,661.

The total cost of those reduced payments—roughly $9,300 over two years—is typically funded by the seller as part of the purchase negotiation. The buyer gets lower payments during the first two years, and if interest rates decline during that window, they may have the opportunity to refinance into a permanently lower rate before year three arrives.

In slower housing markets, temporary buydowns are sometimes used as a way for sellers to make a property more attractive without reducing the purchase price.

Turning Seller Motivation into Buyer Savings

I worked with a couple purchasing their first home during a period when mortgage rates were hovering near 7 percent. They had found a home they loved in Williamson County, but when we calculated the full monthly payment, the number gave them pause. It wasn't that they couldn't afford it. It was that the payment felt heavier than they had imagined when they started their search.

The home had been on the market for several weeks, and the seller was motivated to close. In a situation like that, many buyers instinctively ask for a price reduction. But we took a different approach.

Instead of negotiating the price down, we asked the seller to fund a 2-1 temporary rate buydown as part of the purchase agreement. The seller agreed. From the seller's perspective, it was a better outcome than cutting the sale price—the purchase price stayed intact, which preserved the comparable sale value for the neighborhood, and the total cost of funding the buydown was less than the price reduction the buyers would have otherwise requested.

For the buyers, the impact was immediate. During year one, their effective interest rate dropped to 5 percent, saving them more than $500 per month. In year two, the rate moved to 6 percent, still saving them roughly $250 per month compared to the full note rate.

But the real advantage came fourteen months into the loan. Mortgage rates had declined meaningfully from where they were at the time of purchase. Because the buyers had preserved their cash instead of paying discount points upfront, they were in a strong position to refinance into a new loan at a permanently lower rate—just before the buydown period ended.

No single piece of that strategy was complicated. But each decision—choosing a buydown over a price reduction, preserving liquidity, watching for the right refinance window—was intentional. And together, they saved the buyers tens of thousands of dollars over the first several years of ownership.

Structure Matters More Than Rate Alone

Mortgage points and buydowns illustrate an important idea. A mortgage isn't defined by a single number. It's defined by how the loan is structured. The right decision depends on your timeline, your liquidity, and your long-term financial plans.

14

WHAT HAPPENS AFTER YOU GO UNDER CONTRACT

FOR MANY HOMEBUYERS, THE MOMENT THEIR OFFER IS ACCEPTED feels like the finish line. In reality, the mortgage process is just entering its most active phase.

From the time a purchase contract is signed until the day you close on the home, several important steps take place behind the scenes. Understanding what's coming makes the whole thing feel far more predictable.

One of the first things that happens after your offer is accepted is the earnest money deposit. This is a good-faith payment—typically 1 percent of the purchase price—that the buyer submits to demonstrate serious intent to complete the transaction. The deposit is usually held in an escrow account managed by the title company or closing attorney.

Earnest money is not an additional cost. At closing, it is applied toward your down payment or closing costs. But it matters because the terms surrounding it affect your risk. If the transaction closes successfully, the deposit simply becomes part of your purchase funds. If the deal falls apart for a reason covered by one of your contract contingencies—such as a failed inspection, a low appraisal, or a financing issue—your earnest money is typically refundable. However, if you back out of the deal for reasons not protected by a contingency, you may forfeit the deposit to the seller.

Your real estate agent will typically guide you on how much earnest money to offer based on local customs and market conditions. In competitive markets, a larger deposit can signal stronger commitment to the seller.

Around this same time, most buyers also schedule a home inspection. Inspections are often confused with appraisals, but they serve very different purposes—and it's important to understand the distinction.

The appraisal protects the lender. It confirms that the property is worth the amount being financed. **The inspection protects you.** A licensed home inspector evaluates the physical condition of the property—the roof, foundation, electrical systems, plumbing, HVAC, and other major components—and produces a detailed report of any issues found.

An appraisal can come back at full value even if the roof is nearing the end of its useful life or the electrical panel needs updating. The appraiser is focused on market value, not on whether you'll need to spend $15,000 on repairs within the first year of ownership.

Most purchase contracts include an inspection contingency that gives the buyer a specific window—often seven to fourteen days—to complete the inspection and negotiate any concerns with the seller. If significant issues are discovered, the buyer can request repairs, ask for a price adjustment, or in some cases walk away from the deal.

The inspection is not required by the lender, and buyers are free to waive it. In competitive markets, some buyers choose to do so in order to strengthen their offer. But waiving the inspection means accepting the property as-is, with no recourse if problems surface after closing. For most buyers—especially first-time buyers—the inspection is one of the most important protections available during the purchase process.

Step 1: Loan Application and Initial Disclosures

Once a purchase contract is fully executed, the lender begins preparing the official loan application and required disclosures. These outline key details about the loan, including the estimated interest rate, monthly payment, closing costs, and loan terms.

Federal regulations require lenders to provide these documents within a specific timeframe. Borrowers will typically review and electronically sign the disclosures to acknowledge receipt. This stage is largely about transparency—ensuring borrowers clearly understand the loan structure before the process moves forward.

Two Details That Catch Buyers Off Guard

Two details that often catch buyers off guard during this stage are rate locks and closing costs, so it's worth understanding both before you encounter them.

A rate lock is an agreement between you and the lender that freezes your interest rate for a specific period—typically thirty to sixty days—while the loan is being processed. This protects you from rate increases during that window. A longer lock gives you more breathing room if the closing gets delayed, but it may come at a slightly higher rate. Your lender should help you choose the lock period that balances protection with cost.

If your loan closes within the lock period, you get the locked rate regardless of what happens in the market. If the lock expires before closing—because of processing delays, for example—you may need to extend it, which can sometimes involve an additional fee. Your lender should discuss timing and lock strategy early in the process.

Closing costs are the fees associated with finalizing the mortgage and transferring ownership. On a typical purchase, closing costs generally range from 2 to 4 percent of the loan amount. On a $400,000 loan, that means roughly $8,000 to $16,000.

These costs typically include lender fees (origination, underwriting, processing), third-party fees (appraisal, title search, title insurance, attorney or closing agent fees), prepaid items (homeowners insurance, property taxes, and prepaid interest), and government recording fees.

Your lender is required to provide a Loan Estimate within three business days of your application. This document breaks down the estimated closing costs in detail. Reviewing it carefully—and comparing it to the final Closing Disclosure before signing—is one of the most important things you can do during the process.

Step 2: Loan Processing

Once the disclosures are signed, the loan file moves into processing. The processor collects documentation, organizes the borrower's financial information, and prepares the file for underwriting review.

During this stage, borrowers may be asked to provide updated bank statements, pay stubs, explanations for certain deposits or credit inquiries, and additional documentation related to employment or assets.

Many buyers are surprised by how detailed these requests get. But lenders are required to carefully document your financial profile—which is exactly why early preparation pays off.

Shopping for Homeowners Insurance

One task that often gets left until the last minute is securing homeowners insurance. Most lenders require proof of insurance before they will issue a clear to close, so waiting too long can create unnecessary stress at the end of the process.

During loan processing, it is worth getting quotes from several insurance providers. Premiums can vary significantly depending on the insurer, the property's location, the age of the home, and the coverage limits you select.

At a minimum, your policy should cover the cost of rebuilding the home in the event of a total loss—not just the purchase price. Your lender will have specific coverage requirements, and your insurance agent can help you understand what is and isn't included in a standard policy. Flood insurance, for example, is typically a separate policy and may be required if the property is in a designated flood zone.

Starting this process early gives you time to compare options and avoid overpaying—and it prevents a last-minute scramble that can delay your closing.

Step 3: Appraisal

While the loan is moving through processing, the lender will typically order an appraisal of the property. The appraiser compares the property to similar homes that have recently sold and considers factors such as square footage, location, condition, and recent comparable sales.

If the home appraises at or above the purchase price, the transaction can usually move forward. If the appraisal comes in lower, the buyer and seller may need to negotiate how to address the difference. We will discuss this situation further in Chapter 16.

Step 4: Underwriting

Once the loan file has been fully prepared, it is submitted to underwriting. Underwriters review the entire file to confirm that the loan meets the required guidelines.

Sometimes the underwriter will approve the loan immediately. More often, the approval comes with a list of conditions—additional items that must be clarified before the loan can move forward. These might include updated bank statements, written explanations of certain transactions, verification of employment, or documentation of insurance.

A list of conditions can feel intimidating, but it's completely normal. Most loans go through one or two rounds of conditions before final approval.

The Deposits Nobody Expected to Explain

Everything about the file looked straightforward—solid income, clean credit, a first-time buyer in the Nashville area ready to close. Then underwriting flagged something no one expected.

During the document review, we noticed several large deposits in the borrower's bank account that required explanation. The deposits were legitimate—transfers from a side business—but because they hadn't been clearly documented, underwriting couldn't simply assume their source.

The solution was simple. The borrower provided documentation showing the deposits were business transfers, along with a short written explanation. Once added to the file, the underwriter cleared the condition and the loan moved forward.

For first-time buyers, moments like this feel stressful. But they're not unusual. Most underwriting questions are just part of the verification process.

The Financial Freeze: What to Avoid Before Closing

One important detail many buyers don't realize is that their financial profile continues to be monitored during the underwriting process. Lenders typically recommend avoiding major financial changes before closing—opening new credit accounts, financing vehicles or large purchases, making large unexplained deposits, or changing jobs without discussing it with the lender.

Even small changes can sometimes affect how a loan is evaluated. The safest approach is to keep your balance sheet as stable as possible until the loan closes.

Step 5: Clear to Close

Once all underwriting conditions have been satisfied, the loan receives "**Clear to Close**." The closing documents are prepared and sent to the closing agent or title company. Borrowers receive a Closing Disclosure outlining the final loan terms and closing costs.

Federal regulations require that borrowers receive this document at least three business days before signing, giving them time to review the final numbers.

Step 6: Closing Day

Closing day is when the loan documents are signed, the funds are transferred, and ownership of the property officially changes hands. While the number of documents can seem overwhelming, most closing appointments are quite straightforward and typically take less than an hour.

After the documents are signed and the loan is funded, the home officially becomes yours.

15
UNDERSTANDING YOUR CLOSING DOCUMENTS

DURING THE MORTGAGE PROCESS, YOU'LL ENCOUNTER SEVERAL documents that affect how much you pay, what you owe, and what protections you have as a homeowner. Most buyers glance at these, sign where they're told, and move on.

Taking a few minutes to understand what's in front of you can prevent confusion, catch errors, and eliminate one of the most common sources of stress during the first year of homeownership.

The Two Documents You Should Actually Read

Two of the most important documents you'll receive during the mortgage process are the **Loan Estimate** and the **Closing Disclosure**. They contain much of the same information, but they arrive at different points in the timeline—and comparing them is one of the smartest things you can do as a borrower.

The Loan Estimate arrives within three business days of submitting your loan application. It provides a detailed breakdown of your estimated interest rate, monthly payment, closing costs, and loan terms. Think of it as the lender's initial proposal.

The Closing Disclosure arrives at least three business days before your closing date. It reflects the final, actual terms of the loan. By this point, the numbers should be very close to what appeared on the Loan Estimate—but not always identical.

When you receive the Closing Disclosure, compare it to your original Loan Estimate and pay attention to a few key areas:

- **The interest rate and monthly payment** should match what you locked in with your lender. If they don't, ask why.
- **Loan costs**—including origination fees, discount points, and underwriting fees—should be very close to the original estimate. Federal regulations limit how much certain fees can increase between the Loan Estimate and Closing Disclosure.
- **Third-party fees**—such as the appraisal, title search, and title insurance—may shift slightly, but significant changes should be explained.
- **Prepaid items and escrow deposits**—including property taxes, homeowners insurance, and prepaid interest—can vary based on your closing date and local tax schedules. These differences are normal but worth reviewing.
- **The cash to close figure** at the bottom of the Closing Disclosure tells you exactly how much money you need to bring to the closing table. Confirm this number with your lender at least a day before closing so there are no surprises.

You don't need to become an expert in these documents. But taking thirty minutes to compare the two—or asking your lender to walk you through the differences—can prevent confusion and catch errors before they become problems.

Why Your Fixed-Rate Payment Can Still Change

After closing, many buyers are surprised when their mortgage payment changes—even though they have a fixed-rate loan.

This usually has nothing to do with the interest rate. It has to do with escrow.

Most mortgage lenders require borrowers to maintain an escrow account—sometimes called an impound account—as part of the loan. Each month, a portion of your mortgage payment is set aside in this account to cover property taxes and homeowners insurance when they come due.

Instead of paying your annual property tax bill and insurance premium in large lump sums, the lender collects a fraction of those costs each month and pays them on your behalf.

Here's where the confusion comes in: property taxes and insurance premiums change over time. When your county reassesses your property value and raises your tax bill, or when your insurance premium increases at renewal, your escrow payment adjusts to reflect those new amounts.

That means your total monthly mortgage payment can go up—even though your principal and interest remain exactly the same.

This surprises a lot of first-time buyers. The key is understanding that the fixed portion of your payment—principal and interest—never changes on a fixed-rate loan. But the escrow portion fluctuates based on taxes and insurance.

Once a year, your lender will perform an escrow analysis to determine whether your account is collecting enough to cover upcoming expenses. You'll receive a letter from your lender once a year showing the results of this analysis. If your payment is changing, this letter explains why. It's worth reading—not because you need to take action, but because it prevents the surprise of seeing a different number on your mortgage statement. If there's a shortfall, your monthly payment will increase. If there's a surplus, you may receive a small refund.

Understanding this upfront prevents one of the most common sources of confusion during the first year of homeownership.

The One-Time Insurance Most Buyers Overlook

During the closing process, you'll see a line item for title insurance. Many buyers glance at it, assume it's required, and move on. But it's worth understanding what you're paying for—because there are actually two types, and only one of them protects you.

Title insurance exists to protect against problems with the ownership history of the property. Before closing, a title company conducts a title search—reviewing public records to confirm that the seller actually has clear legal ownership of the home and that there are no outstanding liens, claims, or disputes attached to it.

Most of the time, the search comes back clean. But occasionally, issues surface: unpaid contractor liens, errors in prior legal documents, undisclosed heirs, or boundary disputes that were never resolved. Title insurance protects against these kinds of risks.

Here are the important distinctions:

A lender's title policy is almost always required. It protects the lender's interest in the property. If a title issue arises after closing, this policy covers the lender—not you.

An owner's title policy is optional but strongly recommended. It protects your ownership interest. If someone later makes a legal claim against the property—a previously unknown lien, a forged document in the chain of title, or an ownership dispute—the owner's policy covers your legal defense and potential financial loss.

The owner's policy is a one-time cost paid at closing, typically ranging from a few hundred to a couple thousand dollars depending on the purchase price. Unlike most insurance, you pay for it once and it covers you for as long as you own the home.

Many buyers skip the owner's policy to save money at closing. In most transactions, nothing goes wrong. But when a title issue does surface months or years later, the cost of resolving it without insurance can be significant. For the relatively modest one-time premium, it's generally worth the protection.

When Your Loan Changes Hands

Shortly after closing, some homeowners receive a letter informing them that their mortgage has been transferred to a different company. This can feel unsettling—especially if you chose your lender carefully and suddenly find yourself making payments to a company you've never heard of.

This is completely normal. As we discussed earlier in the book, most mortgages are sold into the secondary market after closing. When that happens, the servicing of the loan—collecting payments, managing the escrow account, and handling customer inquiries—is often transferred to a separate mortgage servicer.

The transfer does not change your loan terms. Your interest rate, monthly payment, remaining balance, and loan structure all stay exactly the same. What changes is where you send the payment and who you call with questions.

When you receive a servicing transfer notice, pay attention to three things: the new servicer's name and contact information, the date your first payment is due to the new servicer, and confirmation that your loan terms have not changed. Federal law requires both the old and new servicers to notify you in writing, and there is typically a grace period during the transition where a payment sent to the wrong servicer will not be counted as late.

16
WHEN THE APPRAISAL DOESN'T MATCH THE PRICE

FOR MOST HOMEBUYERS, THE PURCHASE PRICE OF THE HOME FEELS like the final answer. But during the mortgage process, there is one more opinion that matters: the appraiser's.

The appraisal is the lender's way of confirming that the property is worth the amount being financed. Because the home serves as collateral for the loan, the lender needs to make sure the value supports the transaction.

What the Appraiser Is Actually Looking For

An appraisal is performed by a licensed appraiser who is independent of both the buyer and the lender. The appraiser evaluates the property and compares it to similar homes—called "**comps**"—that have recently sold in the same area.

The appraiser looks at factors such as square footage, location, condition, recent comparable sales, and market trends in the neighborhood.

If the appraised value matches or exceeds the contract price, the loan process continues normally. But occasionally, the appraised value comes in lower.

When the Appraiser's Number Doesn't Match Yours

Appraisals are based primarily on recent comparable sales, which means they often reflect what homes sold for in the recent past. In rapidly changing markets, contract prices may move faster than comparable sales data.

This can create situations where a buyer and seller agree on a price that reflects current demand, while the appraisal reflects slightly older data. The difference doesn't necessarily mean the home isn't worth the price—it simply means the appraiser must rely on documented comparable sales to support the value.

Your Options When the Numbers Don't Agree

When an appraisal comes in below the contract price, the lender will typically limit the loan amount to the appraised value. That creates a gap between what the lender will finance and what you agreed to pay. At that point, you generally have four paths forward.

1. **Renegotiate the purchase price.** The most straightforward approach is to ask the seller to lower the price to match the appraised value. Some sellers will agree, particularly if the home has been on the market for a while or if they're motivated to close quickly. Others won't—especially in competitive markets where they believe another buyer will pay the original price. Your real estate agent can help you determine how much leverage you have based on the seller's situation.

2. **Split the difference.** In many cases, neither the buyer nor the seller wants to walk away. A common compromise is to meet somewhere in the middle—the seller reduces the price by a portion of the gap, and the buyer covers the rest. This keeps the transaction moving without either side absorbing the full impact.
3. **Bring additional cash to cover the gap.** If you believe the home is worth the contract price despite the appraisal, you can choose to pay the difference out of pocket. The lender will finance based on the appraised value, and you cover the gap with additional funds at closing. This is essentially what appraisal gap coverage commits you to in advance. It's a viable option when you have the reserves and the confidence that the home's value supports the price—but it does mean tying up more cash in the property.
4. **Walk away from the transaction.** If the gap is too large and no compromise can be reached, the buyer can cancel the contract. Most purchase agreements include an appraisal contingency that protects the buyer's earnest money in this situation. Without that contingency, walking away could mean forfeiting your deposit. This is why understanding your contract contingencies before you make an offer matters—it determines how much flexibility you have if the numbers don't line up.

The Offer Strategy That Won Without the Highest Price

The home was listed at $1.05 million in Franklin, and the buyers—relocating from out of state—were told it would attract multiple offers. The buyers were comfortable offering above asking, but they had one concern: *What would happen if the home didn't appraise for the full contract price?*

Instead of simply hoping the appraisal would come in high enough, we discussed structured **appraisal gap coverage**. Appraisal gap coverage is simply a commitment from the buyer to cover the difference—using their own funds—between what the appraiser says the home is worth and what the buyers agreed to pay. It tells the seller: even if the appraisal comes in low, I'm prepared to make up the gap, up to a limit.

This structure gave the seller confidence that the deal would still close even if the appraisal came in slightly lower. Their offer wasn't actually the highest one submitted, but because the financing was structured to reduce uncertainty, it was ultimately accepted.

And in an interesting twist, the home eventually appraised for approximately $1.2 million, meaning the gap coverage never came into play. But the strategy itself helped them secure the home.

When Confidence Matters as Much as Price

Sellers want certainty. They want confidence that your financing will close smoothly and on time. Once you see how mortgage structure interacts with appraisal risk, you can craft a much stronger offer.

Sometimes that confidence can matter just as much as price.

PART IV
Special Situations, Strategy, and Planning

17
THE CHALLENGE OF SELF-EMPLOYED BORROWERS

FOR MANY ENTREPRENEURS AND BUSINESS OWNERS, APPLYING FOR a mortgage can feel surprisingly frustrating.

From the outside, their financial situation may look strong. The business generates healthy revenue, cash flow is solid, and they may even have substantial assets. Yet when they apply for a mortgage, they sometimes hear: "You don't qualify." Or worse: "You'll need to wait a couple of years."

This happens far more often than people realize. And the reason usually has nothing to do with how successful the business is. It's about **how income is documented**.

Why a Profitable Business Can Look Broke on Paper

Traditional mortgage underwriting was designed primarily for borrowers with predictable W-2 income. Pay stubs, W-2 forms, and employment verification provide a clear picture of what the borrower earns.

Self-employed income works differently. Business owners often deduct legitimate business expenses to reduce their taxable income. Accountants do this intentionally as part of responsible tax planning.

The result is that a business owner who generates significant revenue may report much lower income on their tax returns. From a tax perspective, that can be beneficial. From a mortgage underwriting perspective, it can create challenges—because traditional guidelines rely heavily on taxable income.

The Averaging Trap

Most conventional mortgage programs require lenders to review two years of tax returns for self-employed borrowers. The lender typically calculates income by averaging those two years of reported earnings.

But deductions can significantly reduce those numbers. For example, depreciation, vehicle expenses, and other business deductions may reduce taxable income even though the business itself produces strong cash flow.

Two Banks Said No

Two banks had already said no. The business owner's revenue was strong, his cash flow was healthy, and he had plenty of assets—but his tax returns told a very different story, and that was all the previous lenders had looked at.

Both lenders concluded that his income wasn't high enough to qualify for the home he wanted to purchase. The frustrating part was that the business itself was doing very well. His accountant had simply done an excellent job minimizing taxable income through legitimate deductions. When this situation occurs, we often pivot to alternative documentation loans.

Alternative Documentation Loans

Instead of relying solely on tax returns, some loan programs allow lenders to evaluate income using alternative forms of documentation. One of the most common options is called a bank statement loan.

Rather than analyzing taxable income on tax returns, these loans review the deposits flowing into the borrower's business bank accounts over a specific period—often twelve or twenty-four months.

In this borrower's case, we gathered twelve months of business bank statements and analyzed the deposits. The pattern demonstrated consistent and healthy cash flow. Using that documentation, the borrower was able to qualify for the loan and close on the home within about thirty days.

What two banks had described as impossible turned out to be a solvable problem once the right loan structure was used.

Why Different Lenders Give You Different Answers

Different lenders specialize in different types of loans. Some focus primarily on traditional W-2 borrowers. Others have access to programs designed for business owners, investors, or borrowers with more complex financial profiles.

This is why you can get completely different answers from different lenders. It's not always that one is right and the other wrong. One may simply have access to tools the other doesn't.

Small Moves That Make a Big Difference

For self-employed borrowers, preparation can make a significant difference:

- Keeping business and personal finances well-organized
- Maintaining clear documentation of deposits and revenue

- Discussing upcoming home purchases with your accountant in advance
- Avoiding unusually large deductions right before applying for a mortgage

You're not trying to manipulate anything. You're simply understanding how your financial decisions interact with mortgage guidelines.

18

WHEN LIFE CHANGES

Mortgages During Major Transitions

MOST PEOPLE ASSOCIATE MORTGAGES WITH ONE SPECIFIC EVENT: buying a home. But over the years, I've learned that mortgages often become most important during major life transitions.

Relocations, career changes, growing families, downsizing, or divorce can all create situations where the structure of a mortgage plays a critical role in determining what options are available. These moments tend to be emotional, fast-moving, and full of competing priorities. That combination makes it easy to default to the simplest available option rather than the one that actually fits.

The stories in this chapter come from buyers navigating some of the most stressful periods of their lives. In each case, the mortgage was not the main event. But how it was structured made everything else either harder or easier.

When Divorce Doesn't Mean Selling the Home

One of the more emotional situations I've worked through involved a couple going through a divorce. They owned a home in Franklin with nearly $400,000 in equity, and both initially assumed the house would need to be sold so they could divide the proceeds.

Their attorney believed selling was the only realistic option because both spouses were listed on the existing mortgage. But one spouse strongly hoped to remain in the home. For them, the house represented stability for their children during an already difficult time.

When we reviewed the situation more closely, we realized there was another option. Instead of selling, we structured a divorce buyout refinance. The spouse keeping the home refinanced the existing mortgage into their name alone, and the new loan included additional funds to buy out the other spouse's share of equity.

Here's how it worked in simple terms. The home was worth roughly $800,000 and the existing mortgage balance was around $400,000, leaving about $400,000 in equity. Each spouse was entitled to half of that equity—$200,000. The spouse staying in the home refinanced into a new mortgage of approximately $600,000: the original $400,000 balance plus $200,000 in cash that went to the departing spouse.

One spouse was able to remain in the home with the children. The other received their share of equity in cash to use toward their next chapter. The property never hit the market. The children's lives stayed as stable as possible during an unstable time.

Many people don't realize this type of solution exists. They assume that if both names are on the mortgage, the home must be sold. That's not always true—but it does require a lender who understands how to structure the transaction and coordinate with the attorneys involved.

The Relocation That Almost Fell Apart

Relocations create a timing problem that most buyers don't fully appreciate until they're in the middle of it.

A family moving from Atlanta to the Nashville area had already found the home they wanted. The husband had accepted a new position, their children were registered for school, and they needed to close within forty-five days. But their existing home in Atlanta hadn't sold yet.

That created a financial puzzle. They still had a mortgage payment of roughly $3,200 per month on the Atlanta home. When the new lender calculated their debt-to-income ratio, that existing payment was included—which pushed them over the qualifying threshold for the Nashville purchase.

Their first lender told them they had two options: sell the Atlanta home first, or wait. Neither worked. Waiting meant losing the Nashville home they had already committed to, and a quick sale in Atlanta would likely mean leaving money on the table.

When they came to us, we took a different approach. First, we documented a signed listing agreement showing the Atlanta home was actively on the market at a price supported by comparable sales. Then we worked with a loan program that allowed us to exclude the existing mortgage payment from the DTI calculation based on sufficient equity in the departing property and documentation that the home was listed for sale.

We also structured the Nashville purchase with a slightly smaller down payment than they originally planned. That preserved more cash in reserve—which mattered, because for a period of time they would be carrying costs on two homes.

They closed on the Nashville home on schedule. The Atlanta property sold about six weeks later at a strong price. During those six weeks, the reserves we had preserved covered the overlap comfortably.

If we had simply accepted the first lender's answer, the family would have either lost the home or sold their Atlanta property under pressure. Instead, the right loan structure and a lender familiar with relocation scenarios turned a stressful situation into a manageable one.

When a Career Change Meets a Mortgage Timeline

Not every life transition involves moving to a new city. Sometimes the transition is professional—and the timing can collide with a home purchase in ways buyers don't expect.

A buyer in Williamson County had been planning to purchase a home for several months. His pre-approval was in place, his documentation was organized, and he was actively looking at properties. Then, about three weeks before he expected to make an offer, he received an opportunity he couldn't pass up: a senior role at a new company with a significant increase in compensation.

He assumed the higher income would only help his mortgage application. He was surprised to learn that it actually complicated things.

Mortgage underwriting values stability. When a borrower changes jobs during the loan process, lenders need to re-verify employment and income. If the new role is salaried and in the same industry, the disruption is usually minor. But if the new position involves a probationary period, a shift from salary to commission, or a change in industry, the lender may need to re-evaluate the entire application.

In this case, the new role included a base salary plus performance bonus. The base salary alone was enough to qualify, but the lender couldn't count the bonus income because he had no history of earning it in previous positions. His qualifying income actually went down temporarily, even though his real earning power had gone up.

We worked through it by restructuring the loan around the base salary only and adjusting the target price range slightly to keep the debt-to-income ratio comfortable. He closed on a home about sixty days later. Once he had documented bonus income in the new role, he had the option to use that full income for future purchases.

The lesson wasn't that he should have delayed the career move. It was that the timing of a job change relative to a mortgage application matters—and a conversation with your lender before making that switch can prevent a lot of unnecessary stress.

Planning During Life Transitions

Each of these situations had something in common. The buyers were dealing with circumstances that felt urgent, emotional, and outside their control. In every case, the instinct was to default to the simplest path—sell the house, wait until things settle down, or just take whatever the first lender offers.

But in every case, a more thoughtful approach to the mortgage created options that didn't seem to exist at first.

Life transitions are unpredictable. But once you've seen how mortgages can be structured during these moments, you'll often discover solutions you didn't know were available. Having a lender who has navigated these situations before makes an enormous difference—not just in the loan terms, but in how much stress you carry through an already difficult time.

19
FROM HOMEOWNER TO REAL ESTATE INVESTOR

FOR MOST HOMEBUYERS, A MORTGAGE IS SIMPLY THE TOOL THAT AL-lows them to purchase the home they live in. But over time, many people begin to realize that real estate can also play an important role in building long-term wealth.

Rental properties, vacation homes, and investment properties can generate income, appreciation, and tax advantages when managed properly. And more often than you might expect, mortgages are the financial engine that makes those investments possible.

But the investor mindset doesn't start with your second property. It often starts with how you finance your first one.

The Moment the Thinking Shifts

The plan seemed bulletproof: a buyer relocating to Nashville had just sold a property and intended to purchase the next one entirely with cash. No mortgage, no interest payments, no risk. At least, that was the theory.

But when we looked at their broader financial picture, another perspective emerged. Putting all of their available cash into the home would leave them with very little liquidity and would remove a significant amount of capital from their investment portfolio.

Instead, we discussed using a mortgage to finance a portion of the purchase while keeping a meaningful amount of their capital invested. Historically, the returns they were earning on their investments exceeded the effective cost of the mortgage.

They still made a healthy down payment, but they maintained liquidity and kept their investments working for them.

This buyer wasn't purchasing a rental property. They were buying their primary residence. But the way they structured the financing—borrowing at a lower cost so their capital could work harder elsewhere—was an investor's decision. And that shift in thinking is exactly where real estate investing begins for most people.

The idea behind it has a name: leverage.

Understanding Leverage

Leverage simply means using borrowed money to control a larger asset than you could purchase with cash alone.

Here's a simple example.

Imagine purchasing a $500,000 property with a 20 percent down payment. You contribute $100,000 of your own money. The mortgage covers the remaining $400,000.

Now imagine the property appreciates by 5 percent over the next year. The home is now worth $525,000—a $25,000 increase. But you didn't invest $500,000. You invested $100,000. That means your $25,000 gain represents a 25 percent return on the money you actually put in, before accounting for expenses.

That's the power of leverage. A modest increase in the property's value translates into a much larger return on your invested capital because the mortgage allowed you to control a $500,000 asset with $100,000.

But leverage works in both directions, and this is important to understand before going further.

Imagine that same $500,000 property declines in value by 10 percent. The home is now worth $450,000, but you still owe close to $400,000 on the mortgage. Your $100,000 in equity has been cut in half—a 50 percent loss on your original investment, even though the property only dropped 10 percent.

If the property also has negative cash flow—meaning the rent doesn't fully cover the mortgage, taxes, insurance, and maintenance—those losses add up month after month. And unlike a stock you can sell with a few clicks, you can't sell a property overnight if conditions change.

This is why successful real estate investors don't just chase appreciation. They focus on cash flow, reserves, and planning for the unexpected. If that sounds familiar, it should. The same principle we discussed with your primary residence—don't drain your savings for the down payment—applies even more directly when you're investing.

The Most Natural Path Into Investing

Many buyers assume that real estate investing is something separate from the home-buying process—a future project that requires a completely different set of tools and knowledge. In reality, the transition from homeowner to investor is often much smaller than people expect.

One of the most common paths into real estate investing begins with a home you've already purchased.

I've worked with several buyers over the years who purchased their first home, lived in it for a few years, and then—when they were ready to move into a larger home or relocate—chose to keep the original property as a rental instead of selling it.

The math often works in their favor. By the time they're ready to move, the original mortgage payment is typically lower than current market rents, especially if they purchased when rates were favorable. The home may have appreciated, giving them a cushion of equity. And because they've lived in the property, they understand its condition, its maintenance needs, and its neighborhood better than any outside investor would.

This isn't an exotic investment strategy. It's one of the most natural ways people build rental income over time.

The Duplex Strategy

Another path that's become increasingly popular—particularly among younger buyers—is purchasing a small multi-unit property, such as a duplex or triplex, as a primary residence. The buyer lives in one unit and rents out the others. In many cases, the rental income covers a significant portion of the mortgage payment, dramatically reducing the buyer's effective housing cost.

What makes this approach especially accessible is that owner-occupied multi-unit properties—up to four units—can typically be financed using the same loan programs available for single-family homes. That means FHA loans with 3.5 percent down, conventional loans with 5 percent down, or VA loans with zero down for eligible borrowers.

You don't need to be a seasoned investor to take this step. But you do need to think about the purchase strategically from the beginning—understanding how rental income factors into your qualification, what reserves you'll want to maintain, and how the property fits into your longer-term plans.

When Leverage Isn't the Right Move

Before we go any further, I want to be direct about when investing with a mortgage is not the right decision.

Leverage works best when cash flow is strong, reserves are deep, and the investor has the financial stability to absorb surprises. When any of those conditions are missing, the risks increase significantly.

Borrowers with thin cash reserves are particularly vulnerable. Investment properties come with vacancies, repairs, and unexpected expenses—just like primary residences, but often with less predictability. If you're stretching to make the down payment on an investment property and have little left afterward, one bad month can create serious financial pressure.

Unstable or unpredictable income is another warning sign. If your earnings fluctuate significantly from year to year, taking on additional mortgage obligations may limit your flexibility at exactly the moment you need it most.

And perhaps most importantly, the decision to invest should be based on your own numbers—not someone else's success story. Buying a rental property because a friend did well with one, or because social media makes it look easy, is not a strategy. The investors I've seen succeed over time are the ones who run the numbers carefully, plan for downside scenarios, and make decisions based on their actual financial situation.

If you're not sure whether you're in a position to invest, that uncertainty is worth exploring with both your lender and a financial advisor before committing.

From Homeowner to Investor

The transition from owning one home to owning an investment property is one of the most significant financial steps many people take. When it's done thoughtfully—with realistic expectations, adequate reserves, and a mortgage structure that supports the plan—it can be the beginning of meaningful wealth building.

The next chapter explores what happens when investors are ready to go beyond that first property and begin building a portfolio.

20

SCALING A REAL ESTATE PORTFOLIO WITH MORTGAGES

FOR INVESTORS WHO HAVE PURCHASED THEIR FIRST RENTAL PROPERTY and seen how the math works, a natural question follows: *How do I do this again?*

Scaling a real estate portfolio is where mortgage strategy becomes especially important. The loan programs that work well for your first or second investment property may not be available—or may not be the best fit—as your portfolio grows. Understanding how financing options evolve as you scale is one of the most important things an investor can learn.

When Conventional Financing Hits a Wall

Traditional conventional loan guidelines typically allow borrowers to finance up to ten properties. For your first few investment purchases, conventional loans often provide competitive rates and familiar qualification requirements.

But as the portfolio grows, each additional mortgage increases the borrower's total debt obligations. Lenders evaluate all of those obligations when calculating the debt-to-income ratio, which means qualifying for property number seven or eight can be significantly more difficult than qualifying for property number two—even if every existing property is cash-flowing well.

For many investors, that limit eventually becomes a barrier.

The Investor Who Was Told to Stop

An investor relocating from Chicago had built an impressive rental portfolio—and was about to hit a wall. He was approaching the conventional ten-loan limit, and none of his previous lenders had ever mentioned what comes next.

He assumed he was done. The banks he had been working with didn't offer anything beyond conventional financing for investment properties, so the message he kept hearing was: you've maxed out.

That's when we explored a different type of loan—one designed specifically for this situation.

How DSCR Loans Work

A DSCR loan—which stands for Debt Service Coverage Ratio loan—is an investment property loan that qualifies the property rather than the borrower's personal income.

Here's what that means in plain language.

With a conventional mortgage, the lender looks at how much money you earn, adds up all your monthly debts, and decides whether you can afford another payment. With a DSCR loan, the lender asks a different question: *Does this specific property generate enough rental income to cover its own mortgage payment?*

The lender calculates a simple ratio. Take the property's expected monthly rent and divide it by the total monthly housing cost—which includes the mortgage payment, property taxes, insurance, and any HOA fees.

Here's an example. Suppose a rental property generates $2,500 per month in rent. The total monthly cost of owning the property—mortgage, taxes, insurance, and HOA—comes to $2,000. Dividing rent by cost gives you 1.25. That means the rent exceeds the payment by 25 percent. The property is more than paying for itself.

That number—1.25—is the DSCR. Most lenders look for a ratio of at least 1.0, meaning the rent covers the full payment. Better rates and terms are typically available at 1.25 or higher because the additional cushion reduces the lender's risk.

For the Chicago investor, this structure opened the door to acquiring additional rental properties without needing to dramatically increase his personal income or liquidate other investments. The key insight was understanding that the financing structure needed to evolve as the investment strategy evolved.

Tax Advantages Worth Understanding

One of the reasons real estate investors frequently choose to finance properties rather than pay cash is the tax treatment of mortgage interest and property ownership. This book is not a tax guide, and you should always consult a qualified tax professional about your specific situation. But a few concepts are worth understanding at a high level because they directly influence the financing decision.

- **The first is the mortgage interest deduction.** On investment properties, the interest you pay on the mortgage is generally deductible as a business expense. Think of it this way: if you're paying 7 percent interest on a mortgage, but a portion of that interest reduces your taxable income, the actual cost of borrowing—what it's really costing you after the tax benefit—is lower than 7 percent. The exact amount depends on your tax situation, which is why a tax professional matters here.

- **The second is depreciation.** The IRS allows property owners to deduct a portion of the property's value each year as an expense—even though you haven't actually spent that money and even though the property may be going up in value. It's a paper expense that reduces the taxes you owe on rental income. For many investors, depreciation is one of the most significant tax benefits of owning real estate.
- **The third is the 1031 exchange.** When an investor sells a rental property, they normally owe capital gains tax on the profit. But a 1031 exchange allows the investor to defer that tax by reinvesting the proceeds into another investment property. In simple terms, instead of paying taxes on the sale and investing what's left, you roll the full amount into the next property. This allows portfolios to grow without large tax events slowing things down.

These advantages don't make every real estate investment a good one. But they help explain why experienced investors so often choose to use financing rather than tying up all of their capital in a single property.

Mortgages as Strategic Tools

When used strategically, mortgages can be tools for creating opportunity. The ability to control valuable assets, maintain liquidity, and structure debt thoughtfully can allow individuals to grow their wealth in ways that extend far beyond a single home purchase.

Leverage cuts both ways. Real estate markets fluctuate, expenses arise, and every investment carries risk. But when mortgages are paired with long-term strategy—and approached with the same discipline we've discussed throughout this book—those decisions compound into real financial progress.

The key isn't whether to use leverage. It's whether you're using it intentionally.

21

REFINANCING STRATEGY

When It Actually Makes Sense

MOST HOMEOWNERS THINK REFINANCING ONLY MATTERS WHEN rates drop dramatically. Lower rates are one reason to refinance, but they're far from the only one.

Over time, refinancing can become an important tool for adjusting the structure of your mortgage as your financial situation changes.

The Obvious Reason—and Why It's Not Always Obvious

The most widely recognized reason to refinance is to reduce the interest rate on an existing mortgage. But refinancing is not free. Most refinances involve closing costs that may range from 2 to 5 percent of the loan amount.

Because of these costs, homeowners should evaluate the breakeven period—how long it takes for the monthly savings to recover the upfront costs. If the homeowner expects to keep the loan longer than the breakeven point, the refinance may make financial sense.

Here's what that looks like with real numbers. Imagine a homeowner with a $450,000 mortgage at 7.25 percent. Their current principal and interest payment is approximately $3,070 per month. Rates have dropped, and they can refinance into a new thirty-year loan at 5.75 percent, which would bring the payment down to roughly $2,626—a savings of about $444 per month.

The closing costs on the refinance come to $11,000. To find the breakeven point, divide the cost by the monthly savings: $11,000 divided by $444 equals approximately twenty-five months. If the homeowner expects to stay in the home for at least two more years, the refinance begins producing net savings after that point. Over five years beyond breakeven, those savings add up to more than $26,000.

But the math isn't always that clean. **One detail that often gets overlooked is the loan term reset.** When you refinance a loan you've been paying on for five years into a new thirty-year mortgage, you're restarting the amortization clock. You'll pay interest for a longer total period, which can offset some of the monthly savings. For homeowners who want to avoid extending the timeline, refinancing into a twenty- or twenty-five-year term can preserve the payoff schedule while still capturing a meaningful rate reduction—though the monthly payment won't drop as much.

This is exactly why refinancing decisions should be evaluated in context, not just by comparing the old rate to the new one.

When the Goal Isn't a Lower Rate

Sometimes the goal of refinancing is to change the loan's structure rather than simply lower the rate.

A homeowner who originally selected an adjustable-rate mortgage may later refinance into a fixed-rate loan for long-term stability—particularly if their plans have changed and they now expect to stay in the home longer than they originally anticipated. Others may move from a thirty-year loan to a fifteen- or twenty-year mortgage to accelerate the payoff and build equity faster, especially if their income has increased since the original purchase.

I worked with a homeowner who had taken out a 7/1 ARM when she purchased her home, expecting to sell within five years. Life changed. She got married, had a child, and the home that was supposed to be temporary became the place her family had no intention of leaving. With the adjustable period approaching, she was facing the possibility of rate increases she no longer wanted to think about.

We refinanced her into a thirty-year fixed-rate mortgage. Her new rate was slightly higher than what she had been paying during the ARM's fixed period, but the payment was predictable for the life of the loan. For her, the peace of mind was worth more than the modest increase in monthly cost. She didn't refinance because rates dropped. She refinanced because her life had changed and the original loan structure no longer matched her plans.

Turning Your Walls into Working Capital

Another common reason to refinance is to access equity built up in the home. A cash-out refinance allows borrowers to replace their existing mortgage with a larger loan and receive the difference in cash.

Here's what that looks like in practice. Suppose a homeowner has a property worth $600,000 and an existing mortgage balance of

$350,000—meaning they have $250,000 in equity. With a cash-out refinance, they might take out a new mortgage for $450,000. The first $350,000 pays off the original loan. The remaining $100,000 goes to the homeowner as cash.

Those funds can be used for home renovations, debt consolidation, education expenses, business investments, or purchasing additional real estate. I've worked with homeowners who used a cash-out refinance to fund the down payment on a rental property—essentially using the equity in their primary residence to begin building an investment portfolio.

But accessing equity through refinancing also increases your mortgage balance and resets your loan term. The homeowner in the example above now owes $450,000 instead of $350,000, and their monthly payment will reflect that larger balance. This is why a cash-out refinance should always be evaluated in context. The question isn't just whether you can access the equity—it's whether what you plan to do with that money creates more value than the additional borrowing costs over time.

Your Mortgage Doesn't Have to Stay the Same for Thirty Years

Refinancing isn't something homeowners need to evaluate constantly. But it is worth reviewing periodically—especially when interest rates shift, home values increase, or personal financial goals change.

Your mortgage doesn't have to remain static for thirty years. When you view refinancing as a strategic decision rather than a reactive one, it becomes another tool in your financial toolkit.

22
THINKING LIKE A MORTGAGE STRATEGIST

AT THE BEGINNING OF THIS BOOK, I SHARED THE STORY OF A BUYER who spent nearly a year trying to achieve the "perfect" credit score before purchasing a home. The difference between their current score and the target translated to less than $40 per month. Meanwhile, home prices in their market had increased significantly.

The lesson had very little to do with credit scores. It had everything to do with how people think about mortgages.

A Mortgage Is a Financial Tool

Throughout this book, we've explored one central idea: a mortgage is not a transaction. It's a financial tool. And like any tool, its effectiveness depends entirely on how you use it.

Structured well, a mortgage preserves your liquidity, creates flexibility, supports investment opportunities, and plays a direct role in building long-term wealth.

Four Questions Worth More Than Any Rate Quote

The simplest thing you can do to improve your mortgage experience?

Ask better questions:

- *How does this loan structure fit my long-term plans?*
- *How much liquidity should I maintain after closing?*
- *How long do I realistically expect to keep this property?*
- *What flexibility will I have if my circumstances change?*

These conversations lead to better decisions. And better decisions lead to better outcomes.

Why This Process Doesn't Have to Feel Mysterious

For most people, buying a home will never become routine. It's an important milestone that deserves careful thought and planning. But it shouldn't feel mysterious.

When you understand how mortgages work—and how these decisions affect your financial life—you gain the confidence to approach the process on your terms. You understand the tradeoffs. You know what questions to ask. And you move forward knowing your mortgage supports the life you're building.

Buying a home will always involve paperwork, numbers, and a series of steps. But behind that process is something much more important: the financial structure you create for your life going forward.

When you begin to think about mortgages strategically rather than transactionally, the entire process changes. You stop reacting to the system and start using it intentionally.

The Couple Who Used the System

I want to close with one more story, because I think it captures what this entire book is about.

About six months before they planned to buy, a couple started a conversation that went differently than most. They weren't in a rush. They didn't have a specific house in mind yet. They simply wanted to understand how the process worked before they were in the middle of it.

That first conversation was different from what I usually hear. Instead of leading with *"What's your rate?"* they asked questions I wish every buyer would ask. *How much liquidity should we keep after closing? What loan structure makes sense if we think we'll move again in seven to ten years? How does this mortgage fit with the rental property we want to buy in a few years?*

Over the following months, we worked through their full financial picture. We reviewed their credit and made a small adjustment that improved their score before they ever submitted an application. We talked through down payment options and landed on a structure that gave them a comfortable payment without draining their reserves. We discussed whether paying points made sense given their timeline—it didn't—and set that money aside instead.

When they found the right home, everything moved quickly. Their pre-approval was fully underwritten. Their offer was clean. The listing agent called me directly, and I was able to confirm that their financing had already been thoroughly reviewed. In a multiple-offer situation, that confidence helped them win the home.

Underwriting was smooth because the documentation had been organized for months. There were no surprises, no last-minute scrambles, no stressful calls about unexplained deposits or missing paperwork.

After closing, the husband sent me a message. He said it was the least stressful major financial decision they had ever made. Not because buying a home is simple—it isn't. But because they understood every step before they took it.

That is what it looks like to think about your mortgage strategically. Not perfection. Not obsessing over every detail. Just walking into the process with a plan, asking the right questions, and making decisions that actually fit your life.

At the beginning of this book, I told you about a buyer who spent a year chasing a perfect credit score and lost far more in rising home prices than the better rate would ever have saved. That buyer was reacting to the system.

The couple in this story used it.

That's the difference.

ABOUT THE AUTHOR

RL HESSON IS THE FOUNDER OF HESSON LOANS, AN INDEPENDENT mortgage brokerage based in Franklin, Tennessee. He works with homebuyers, real estate investors, and relocating professionals to structure mortgage strategies that align with their long-term financial goals.

Before entering the mortgage industry, RL built his career in analytics and executive leadership. He spent several years working in business analytics at Caesars Entertainment, where he helped analyze customer behavior and large-scale business performance. He later served as Chief Information Officer for a rapidly growing behavioral healthcare company, where he oversaw technology systems and infrastructure during a period of significant expansion.

Alongside his corporate career, RL and his wife developed a deep interest in real estate. Over time, they built a portfolio of rental properties and launched multiple businesses connected to the real estate industry, including brokerage, mortgage, title, and insurance ventures. Their real estate brokerage eventually grew to hundreds of agents across multiple states before being acquired by RE/MAX.

Today RL focuses on helping borrowers navigate the mortgage process through Hesson Loans while remaining active in the real estate industry. His background in analytics, investing, and real estate operations gives him a perspective on mortgages that extends beyond the typical loan transaction.

RL lives in Franklin, Tennessee, with his wife Anna Lauren and their two sons. Together they work in both mortgage and residential real estate, helping families navigate one of the most important financial decisions of their lives.

THE MORTGAGE STRATEGY SESSION

THROUGHOUT THIS BOOK, WE'VE DISCUSSED MANY OF THE DECIsions that shape a mortgage: how much to put down, how much to borrow, which loan program to choose, whether to pay discount points, and how long you expect to own the home.

Individually, each of these decisions matters. But the real advantage comes from looking at them together.

Every borrower's situation is unique. Income structure, assets, career trajectory, lifestyle priorities, and long-term goals all influence what the right mortgage structure should look like.

When I begin working with buyers, the first step is usually a conversation focused on understanding the complete balance sheet:

- *What monthly payment feels comfortable for your lifestyle?*
- *How long do you realistically expect to own this home?*
- *How much liquidity do you want to maintain after closing?*
- *Are you planning to invest in real estate in the future?*

- *Do you expect income changes or career transitions in the coming years?*

Once those answers become clear, the mortgage structure usually becomes much easier to design.

If you are preparing to purchase a home and want help structuring your mortgage strategy, you can schedule a mortgage strategy session at: **www.HessonLoans.com**

BONUS MATERIALS

The Homebuyer's Mortgage Checklist

Buying a home involves many moving parts, and most mortgage issues happen because of small, avoidable mistakes. The checklist below summarizes several of the most important steps borrowers can take to help ensure a smooth mortgage experience.

Before Applying for a Mortgage

- Review your credit report and correct any errors
- Avoid opening new credit accounts if possible
- Reduce high credit card balances
- Organize income and asset documentation
- Maintain stable employment whenever possible

Before Making an Offer on a Home

- Obtain a strong pre-approval from a lender
- Confirm a monthly payment that fits your lifestyle
- Understand estimated closing costs
- Maintain adequate cash reserves after closing
- Discuss your long-term plans with your lender

After Going Under Contract

- Provide requested documentation promptly
- Avoid making large financial changes during the process
- Do not open new credit accounts or take on additional debt
- Confirm homeowner's insurance early
- Stay in close communication with your lender and agent

Before Closing

- Review the Closing Disclosure carefully
- Confirm the final funds needed for closing
- Avoid large purchases before closing day
- Bring required identification and documentation
- Ask questions about anything that is unclear

A well-structured mortgage and a smooth closing process usually come down to three things:

1. **Preparation.**
2. **Communication.**
3. **And understanding the steps involved.**

When buyers approach the process with clarity and organization, the experience tends to be far less stressful—and far more successful.

Glossary of Mortgage Terms

Adjustable-Rate Mortgage (ARM): A mortgage with an interest rate that is fixed for an initial period and then adjusts periodically based on market conditions. Common structures include the 5/1 ARM (fixed for five years) and 7/1 ARM (fixed for seven years).

Appraisal: An independent evaluation of a property's market value, conducted by a licensed appraiser. Lenders require appraisals to confirm the home is worth the amount being financed.

Appraisal Gap Coverage: A commitment from the buyer to cover the difference between the appraised value and the contract price using their own funds, up to a specified limit.

Bank Statement Loan: A mortgage program designed for self-employed borrowers that uses bank deposit history rather than tax returns to document income. Typically requires twelve or twenty-four months of business bank statements.

Breakeven Period: The amount of time it takes for monthly savings from a lower interest rate to recover the upfront cost of obtaining that rate, such as through discount points.

Cash-Out Refinance: A type of refinance where the borrower replaces their existing mortgage with a larger loan and receives the difference in cash.

Clear to Close: The final stage of underwriting, indicating that all conditions have been satisfied and the loan is approved for closing.

Closing Costs: Fees associated with finalizing a mortgage transaction, typically ranging from 2 to 4 percent of the loan amount. These include lender fees, third-party fees, prepaid items, and government recording fees.

Closing Disclosure: A document provided at least three business days before closing that outlines the final loan terms, monthly payment, and closing costs. It should be compared to the original Loan Estimate.

Co-Borrower: A person who shares full responsibility for a mortgage and is typically listed on the property's title. The qualification process considers both borrowers' income, assets, and credit.

Co-Signer: A person who takes responsibility for a mortgage debt but does not go on the property's title. Their income and credit help the primary borrower qualify.

Comparable Sales (Comps): Recently sold properties that are similar in size, location, and condition to the home being appraised. Appraisers use comps to determine a property's market value.

Conforming Loan Limit: The maximum loan amount that Fannie Mae and Freddie Mac will purchase. Loans above this limit are classified as jumbo loans. The limit is updated annually and varies by region.

Conventional Loan: A mortgage that is not insured by a government agency. Conventional loans follow guidelines set by Fannie Mae and Freddie Mac and are the most common type of mortgage.

Credit Score: A numerical summary of a borrower's credit history, used by lenders to assess risk. Higher scores generally result in better loan pricing, though small differences between strong scores often have minimal impact on the rate.

Debt Service Coverage Ratio (DSCR): A ratio used in investment property lending that compares a property's rental income to its total monthly housing cost. A DSCR of 1.25 means the rent exceeds the payment by 25 percent.

Debt-to-Income Ratio (DTI): A measure of how much of a borrower's gross monthly income goes toward debt obligations, including the proposed mortgage payment. Most loan programs allow DTI ratios up to approximately 50 percent.

Depreciation: A tax benefit that allows property owners to deduct a portion of a property's value each year as an expense, even if the property is appreciating in market value.

Discount Points: Upfront fees paid at closing to reduce the interest rate on a mortgage. One point typically equals 1 percent of the loan amount.

DSCR Loan: A mortgage designed for investment properties that qualifies the property based on its rental income rather than the borrower's personal income.

Earnest Money: A good-faith deposit made by the buyer after a purchase contract is accepted, typically between 1 and 3 percent of the purchase price. The deposit is held in escrow and applied toward the down payment or closing costs at closing. If the buyer backs out for a reason not covered by a contract contingency, the deposit may be forfeited to the seller.

Equity: The difference between a property's current market value and the amount still owed on the mortgage. Equity increases as the loan balance is paid down and as the property appreciates in value.

Escrow Account: An account maintained by the mortgage lender that collects a portion of each monthly payment to cover property taxes and homeowners insurance when they come due.

Escrow Analysis: An annual review performed by the mortgage servicer to determine whether the borrower's escrow account is collecting enough each month to cover upcoming property tax and insurance payments. If there is a shortfall, the monthly payment may increase. If there is a surplus, the borrower may receive a refund.

FHA Loan: A mortgage insured by the Federal Housing Administration, designed for borrowers who may have smaller down payments or less established credit. FHA loans typically require as little as 3.5 percent down.

Gift Funds: Money contributed by a family member or other approved donor to help cover a borrower's down payment or closing costs. Lenders typically require a signed gift letter confirming that no repayment is expected, along with documentation showing the transfer of funds.

Gross Income: A borrower's total income before taxes and deductions. Lenders use gross income when calculating the debt-to-income ratio, which is why qualifying ratios can be misleading—borrowers live on net income, not gross.

HOA (Homeowners Association): An organization that governs a residential community and collects regular fees from homeowners to cover shared expenses such as landscaping, amenities, and common area maintenance. HOA fees are factored into a borrower's debt-to-income ratio and are included in the monthly housing cost calculation for DSCR loans.

Home Inspection: An evaluation of a property's physical condition performed by a licensed inspector, typically during the period between contract acceptance and closing. The inspection covers major systems including the roof, foundation, electrical, plumbing, and HVAC. Unlike an appraisal, which assesses market value for the lender, the inspection is designed to protect the buyer.

Jumbo Loan: A mortgage that exceeds the conforming loan limit. Jumbo loans often have stricter qualification requirements, including higher credit scores and larger down payments.

Lender Credits: The opposite of discount points—the borrower accepts a slightly higher interest rate in exchange for a reduction in upfront closing costs.

Leverage: Using borrowed money to control a larger asset than you could purchase with cash alone. In real estate, leverage allows an investor to purchase a property with a down payment while financing the remainder.

Liquidity: Access to cash or assets that can be quickly converted to cash. Maintaining liquidity after closing provides a financial cushion for unexpected expenses, repairs, and future opportunities.

Loan Estimate: A document provided within three business days of submitting a loan application that outlines the estimated interest rate, monthly payment, closing costs, and loan terms.

Loan Servicer: The company responsible for collecting monthly mortgage payments, managing the escrow account, and handling borrower inquiries after closing. The servicer may or may not be the same company that originally funded the loan, as servicing rights are frequently transferred in the secondary market.

Mortgage-Backed Securities: Financial products created by bundling large numbers of individual mortgages together and selling shares to institutional investors. The pricing of these securities influences mortgage interest rates.

Mortgage Broker: A licensed professional who works with a network of wholesale lenders to find loan options for borrowers. Brokers do not lend their own money—they match borrowers with the lender and loan structure that best fits their situation.

Net Income: A borrower's income after taxes, insurance, retirement contributions, and other deductions. This is the amount a borrower actually takes home and lives on.

Note Rate: The interest rate stated on the mortgage note—the rate the borrower will ultimately pay once any temporary buydown period ends. In a 2-1 buydown, the note rate is the rate that takes effect in year three.

PMI (Private Mortgage Insurance): Insurance required on conventional loans when the borrower puts down less than 20 percent. PMI protects the lender in case of default and can typically be removed once sufficient equity is built.

Pre-Approval: A thorough review of a borrower's financial situation, including verification of income, assets, credit, and employment. A pre-approval carries significantly more weight than a pre-qualification.

Pre-Qualification: A preliminary estimate of how much a borrower may be able to borrow, typically based on unverified information provided by the borrower.

Principal and Interest: The two components of the fixed portion of a mortgage payment. Principal reduces the loan balance; interest is the cost of borrowing. On a fixed-rate loan, this combined amount never changes, though the escrow portion of the total payment can fluctuate.

Rate Cap: A limit on how much an adjustable-rate mortgage's interest rate can increase at each adjustment and over the life of the loan.

Rate Lock: An agreement between the borrower and lender that freezes the interest rate for a specific period while the loan is being processed.

Reserves: Cash or liquid assets that remain available to the borrower after closing. Lenders view reserves as a safety net that demonstrates the borrower's ability to continue making payments.

Retail Lender: A bank, credit union, or mortgage company that originates loans using its own lending platform and product set. Working with a retail lender means choosing from that single lender's available programs.

Secondary Mortgage Market: The marketplace where lenders sell funded mortgages to investors. This system allows lenders to free up capital and continue making new loans, and it plays a major role in determining mortgage rates.

1031 Exchange: A tax strategy that allows an investor to defer capital gains taxes when selling an investment property by reinvesting the proceeds into another qualifying property.

Temporary Rate Buydown: A financing structure where the interest rate is reduced for a limited period, typically one or two years, before returning to the full note rate. A 2-1 buydown reduces the rate by 2 percent in year one and 1 percent in year two.

Title Insurance: Insurance that protects against problems with a property's ownership history. A lender's policy protects the lender; an owner's policy protects the buyer. The owner's policy is optional but recommended.

Title Search: A review of public records conducted before closing to confirm that the seller has clear legal ownership of the property and that no outstanding liens, claims, or disputes are attached to it.

Underwriting: The process by which a lender evaluates a borrower's financial profile to determine whether the loan meets required guidelines. Underwriters review credit, income, assets, employment, and the property itself before issuing approval.

USDA Loan: A mortgage guaranteed by the U.S. Department of Agriculture, designed to promote homeownership in eligible rural and suburban areas. USDA loans offer no down payment for qualified borrowers but include household income limits and geographic eligibility requirements.

VA Loan: A mortgage guaranteed by the U.S. Department of Veterans Affairs, available to eligible service members, veterans, and certain surviving spouses. VA loans often require no down payment and no monthly mortgage insurance.

ACKNOWLEDGMENTS

TO ANNA LAUREN—MY WIFE, MY BUSINESS PARTNER, AND THE PERSON who has been beside me through every chapter of this journey.

Not just this book, but the twenty-three years of building, risking, learning, and growing that made it possible.

We've built businesses, raised our boys, and spent more late nights than I can count working through ideas, challenges, and what comes next.

Every rental property, every career move, every leap of faith—you've been part of all of it.

This book is a reflection of that shared journey.

Thank you for being my partner in everything that matters.

www.ingramcontent.com/pod-product-compliance
Lightning Source LLC
LaVergne TN
LVHW010947110826
845149LV00015B/3241
* 9 7 9 8 9 9 5 9 0 3 6 0 4 *